# Teddy Bear Century

# Teddy Bear Century

Brian and Donna Gibbs

David & Charles

*This book is dedicated to the memory of Donna's late father,*
*Percival Jack Williams*
*16 March 1922 – 3 November 2000*

A DAVID & CHARLES BOOK

First published in the UK in 2002

Text and designs Copyright © Brian and Donna Gibbs 2002
Photography and layout Copyright © David & Charles 2002
Brian and Donna Gibbs have asserted their right to be identified as authors of this work in accordance
with the Copyright, Designs and Patents Act, 1988.

ISBN 0 7153 1252 9

Executive commissioning editor  Cheryl Brown
Executive art editor  Ali Myer
Project editor  Linda Clements
Book designer  Lisa Forrester
Photography  John Stewart (styled photography)
David Johnson (step photography)

Printed in Hong Kong by Hong Kong Graphics  and Printing Ltd
for David & Charles
Brunel House     Newton Abbot     Devon

# Contents

# Introduction

The teddy bear as we know it today has existed for 100 years, although toy bears were produced in more realistic form as a four-wheeled toy in Germany in the late nineteenth century and probably even earlier in history. This date is almost certainly attributed to the cartoon drawn by Clifford K. Berryman that appeared in *The Washington Post* on 16 November 1902. This cartoon, entitled 'Drawing the line at Mississippi', depicted the refusal of Theodore (Teddy) Roosevelt, the President of the United States, to shoot a bear that had been cornered for him whilst he was on a four-day hunting expedition. Shortly afterwards, Morris Michtom displayed a toy bear in his New York window called 'Teddy's Bear' and the toy became an instant success.

As teddy bears grew in popularity world-wide, so the styles and variations changed to suit each particular period in time. This was often due to economic pressures – from warfare right through to the more affluent times in history when the teddy bear evolved into one of the most popular childhood treasures of everyone's memories.

The aim of this book is to commemorate the 100 years of the teddy bear, to take you through all ten decades of the *Teddy Bear Century* with a fascinating line up of facts about the toy and its major manufacturers, plus of course the bears themselves – a representative teddy bear for each particular decade, incorporating some of the design features of the era. In this book you will find a teddy bear to suit all tastes, with the patterns, full instructions and step-by-step guidance to enable anyone to make the teddy bear of their choice. If you ever wished to own an original teddy bear that you once treasured in your childhood but sadly is no more, the cost would in many cases be rather expensive, even if you could in fact find the bear of your dreams. By using the patterns in this book we give you the chance to re-create those magic memories of the past that are so special to us all.

Whether you are an expert or novice at bear making, there will surely be a teddy bear design or two in this book that will inspire you to start making your very own special collection of teddy bears for you and your family to enjoy. And who knows, perhaps one day these bears will become your family heirlooms.

# Teddy Bear Century

**A fascinating decade-by-decade history of the manufacture of the teddy bear.**

## The first decade

**1902** While on a hunting holiday in Smedes, Mississippi, USA, President Theodore Roosevelt refuses to shoot a bear cub that has been captured for him and tethered to a tree.

**1902** In Giengen, Germany Richard Steiff, nephew of German felt toy maker Margarete, designs a realistic and fully jointed toy bear.

**1903** American Morris Michtom, founder of the Ideal Novelty & Toy Company, after seeing the now famous Clifford Berryman cartoon depicting the Roosevelt hunt, asks permission to name his bear design after the President, resulting in bears now being called 'Teddy' bears.

**1904** The Steiff company introduces its trademark 'Button in Ear'. Initially, this small metal button attached to the left ear was embossed with an elephant. Other versions follow, either left blank or embossed with the Steiff name.

**1906** American company Gund Inc, founded by German immigrant Adolph Gund, produces the first of its teddy designs, having originally made belts, necklaces, novelties and soft toys.

**1907** The Steiff company produces an amazing 975,000 bears during this year after having to expand the factory to meet the huge demand.

**1908** J.K. Farnell & Co produces the first bears in England after being encouraged by Eisenmann & Co, a German company trading from London, and the first to bring teddy bears to England.

**1909** On 9 May, Margarete Steiff dies at the age of sixty-one. The whole town of Giengen, where she was born and established her business, goes into mourning.

## The second decade

**1910** Steiff expands over a three-year period by opening warehouses and appointing agents in several European countries as well as in New York, USA and Sydney, Australia.

**1911** Steiff starts to phase out the black boot button eyes for teddy bears in favour of black or black and brown glass eyes, used from now on in increasing amounts.

**1913** The first bear of the German manufacturer Hermann is believed to have been produced in this year in Neufang, near Sonneberg.

**1914** Due to hostilities between Britain and Germany, German imports to Britain are banned around this time, giving rise to the further development of the British soft toy manufacturing industry.

**1915** Deans and Chad Valley make their first jointed mohair teddy bears.

**1916** A patriotic bear called 'The bear of Russia' is introduced by the British company, Deans. Other manufacturers soon follow this idea.

**1917** World War I causes disruption in the toy industry with many factories being taken over for war work – Steiff, for example, making aeroplane parts and other war-related items.

**1919** The first comic strip bear to appear in a British newspaper is 'Bobby Bear' who appears in the *Daily Herald*.

# The third decade

**1920** 'Rupert Bear' first appears in the *Daily Express* newspaper as a comic strip and continues to do so to this day.

**1922** Due to the continued ban on imports from Germany, many British manufacturers start to establish themselves by supplying the UK market. Many, such as Chad Valley, Merrythought, Farnell, and Deans, are now household names.

**1923** The first bear of the Chiltern 'Hugmee' range is marketed, popularizing the Chiltern name.

**1925** More stable production returns after the war and Steiff evolves new ideas for teddy bears, with light, soft kapok stuffing and blonde mohair plush in seven sizes.

**1926** Steiff's 'Teddy Clown' is on sale – a bear made from yellow mohair sometimes brown-tipped and wearing a clown's hat and a neck ruff.

**1927** J.K. Farnell & Co Ltd extends its factory, introducing the 'Anima' wheeled toy range, which includes a bear.

**1928** The Chad Valley Toy Company builds a new factory at Harbourne Works, near Birmingham, Britain.

**1929** The Wall Street crash in America stifles US bear manufacturing, resulting in low-cost bears being produced called 'stick bears'.

# The fourth decade

**1930** Merrythought Ltd establishes themselves in Ironbridge, Shropshire UK. This site was the birthplace of the industrial revolution in Britain and the Merrythought bear is still made here today.

**1932** Chad Valley establishes the Winnie the Pooh range of toys and games: this is mirrored in the US by Parker Bros, among others.

**1933** Hermann toys exhibit a range of dressed teddy bears at a toy exhibition in Sonneberg, Germany.

**1935** J.K. Farnell opens a new factory employing 300 workers (after the previous factory and all stock was destroyed by fire the year before). There are many new lines along with the re-introduction of their popular 'Alpha' series of bears.

**1936** With the boom in teddy bears, another new factory is built in Merton, south-west London for Deans Rag Book Co.

**1937** British Lines Bros, who at this time is the largest toy manufacturer in the world, launches its 'Pedigree' range of soft toys.

**1938** The often-stated father of the teddy bear, Morris Michtom, dies and his son Benjamin takes over the leadership of the Ideal Novelty & Toy Company.

**1939** As the outbreak of World War II is declared, many European toy factories are closed or forced to divert production to war work.

# The fifth decade

**1940** During World War II many factories cease teddy bear production. Deans makes Mae West life-jackets, Merrythought produces textiles for hospitals and the armed forces and Chad Valley produces children's clothes. In Germany, Steiff starts making munitions while Schuco produces telephone equipment.

**1941** Polyester fibre is invented in England by J.R. Whinfield and J.T. Dickson.

**1942** Wendy Boston, a pioneer for safety in toys, leaves London for Wales and begins making soft toys out of unwanted materials as a hobby. As war ends, she establishes a small shop with a staff of three, selling her toy creations.

**1944** 'Smokey the Bear' is announced as the United States' symbol of forest fire prevention.

**1946** Rationing of toys and materials allows cottage industries to evolve throughout Europe, with toys and bears being made from 'available' materials such as rabbit skins, and alternative stuffings from textile waste.

**1947** Hermann, a German family business, produces its first 'peacetime' teddy bears, which are exhibited at a fair in Leipzig.

**1948** Wendy Boston opens a small factory in Wales and patents the first 'safety eye', using rust-proof nuts and washers to secure them.

# The sixth decade

**1950** Synthetic fibres, such as Dacron, Terylene and Draylon, start to be used commercially and throughout this decade become increasingly popular for making soft toys.

**1951** Australian George Weir establishes Ark Toys in South Africa and imports materials from all over the world to make a range of jointed, mohair teddy bears.

**1952** Everyone's favourite glove-puppet teddy bear, Sooty, first appears on television with Harry Corbett. Harry bought Sooty for 7s 6d (37½p) from a novelty shop on Blackpool's famous pier. The bear's very own TV show followed in 1955. Chad Valley have exclusive rights to manufacture 'Sooty' copies.

**1954** Wendy Boston produces her first fully washable, un-jointed teddy bear. The design is made from nylon plush and is filled with foam rubber chips.

**1954** Karl Theodor Unfricht establishes Grisly Spielwaren GmbH in Germany. All the bears are designed by Luise Unfricht and handmade by all members of the family.

**1955** The Merrythought company introduces an automatic stuffing machine, which speeds up production.

**1957** On Christmas Eve, writer Michael Bond finds a lonely looking teddy bear to give to his wife. They name the bear Paddington, from the nearby train station. Looking for something to write, Michael turns to the bear for inspiration and *A Bear Called Paddington* is published the following year.

# The seventh decade

**1960** The Chad Valley company celebrates its centenary. The fabric Bri-Nylon is registered, and teddy bears using the material are made by Pedigree and Deans.

**1963** A new UK children's comic, *Teddy Bear* is launched.

**1963** Russ Berrie, eventually to become a big name in the soft toy industry, is founded in a converted garage in New Jersey, USA. The company is now known as Applause Inc.

**1964** Craft writer Margaret Hutchings publishes one of the first books on bear making, *Teddy Bears and How To Make Them.*

**1965** Teddy bears with 'all-in-one' foam bodies are introduced. Deans Rag Book Co Ltd changes its name to Deans' Childsplay Toys Ltd.

**1966** Chad Valley continues its acquisition of teddy bear companies by drawing up plans to take over H.G. Stone & Co Ltd, with reorganization of soft toy production going to the Chilterns factory in Pontypool, Wales, UK.

**1967** In England, Donald Campbell makes an attempt on the world water speed record: after the fatal crash, his mascot bear Mr Whoppit (by Merrythought) is retrieved from the surface.

**1968** The J.K. Farnell company, a producer of soft toys and teddy bears from the beginning of the century, is bought by a finance company but The Ideal Novelty & Toy Company becomes a publicly owned firm with expansion in Japan, Germany, UK, Australia, New Zealand and Canada.

# The eighth decade

**1970** Some American doll artists begin to create teddy bears as art objects thereby giving rise to the term 'teddy bear artist', used today to describe a teddy bear creator.

**1971** Ultrasuede is invented in America, the material quickly becoming popular for teddy bear pads and for miniature teddy bear making.

**1972** Gabrielle Designs produces the first 'Paddington Bear' soft toy from Michael Bond's stories.

**1973** Chad Valley undergoes a major restructuring of the business: all but two of the factories close with all soft toy production concentrated at Pontypool in Wales.

**1976** The German company Schuco is sold to Dunbee-Combex-Marx. Unable to compete with the Japanese toy industry, the name 'Schuco' is sold off. It is acquired by George Mangold GmbH & Co who use it to market model cars.

**1977** Merrythought designer Jacqueline Revitt leaves the company after seven years, to rejoin later in 1983.

**1978** The Ideal Novelty & Toy Company celebrates its 75th anniversary with a special-issue teddy bear.

**1979** Safety standards in Britain are updated by the British Standards Institution (BSI) during this the 'International Year of the Child', with many events relating to teddy bears held world-wide.

# The ninth decade

**1980** After a slump in the 1970s, Steiff re-emerges with the launch of replica teddy bears. The Steiff Museum is opened in Giengen, Germany.

**1982** Following on from other manufacturers' success, Merrythought introduces a range of collectors' special edition bears, which are later exported to America by Tide-Ryder Inc.

**1983** Deans celebrates its 80th birthday by issuing an anniversary bear. Bunny Campione introduces teddy bears to Sotheby's Auctions.

**1984** The Ideal Novelty & Toy Co produces a porcelain replica of the first 'Ideal' bear but soon after bears are no longer produced and Hasbro acquires some assets.

**1985** A teddy bear by Steiff is sold at Sotheby's in London and is the first bear to reach over £1000. The success of and demand for old teddies is soon recognized by another world-famous auction house, Christie's of London.

**1986** Jack Wilson, of House of Nisbet, invents the process of making 'distressed' mohair by using a 1904 velvet-crushing machine with Norton (Weaving) Ltd. This process is still used by the same weaving company today.

**1988** Deans goes into voluntary liquidation and after a management buy-out, Neil Miller buys the trading rights to Deans' name and its logo, with wife Barbara as finance director.

**1989** A 1926 Steiff bear called 'Happy' enters the Guinness Book of Records after it is sold at Sotheby's for a record breaking £55,000! Steiff's official history book *Button In Ear* is published.

# The tenth decade

**1990** Merrythought produces a special Diamond Jubilee teddy bear to celebrate the 75th anniversary of the company.

**1991** Deans launches a new range of collectors' bears using replicas of old Deans Rag Book patterns.

**1992** Steiff celebrates ninety years of the teddy bear and its new collectors' bear club is launched.

**1993** Deans, founded in 1903, celebrates its centenary year with an anniversary catalogue.

**1994** Another Steiff bear makes the record books: 'Teddy Girl' is sold by Christie's auction house in London for a staggering £110,000!

**1995** The 75th anniversary of 'Rupert Bear' is celebrated at the Bethnal Green Museum of Childhood, in London.

**1997** *Making Traditional Teddy Bears* by Brian and Donna Gibbs is published.

**1998** Michael Bond's 'Paddington Bear' celebrates his 40th birthday.

**1999** Anniversary of the death of Marguerite Steiff, the person who gave us the household name for the 'definitive teddy bear'.

**1999** As we exit this decade, soon to start a new millennium, teddy bears have proved to be the favourite toy for a whole century of children.

# Materials and Equipment

There is a vast array of materials and components to choose from when making teddy bears and this section is intended to guide you through the choices you can make. There is useful information on choosing fabrics, fillings and threads, selecting eyes, noses and joints, and descriptions of some of the tools you may need. If you intend to make a bear for a child, it is imperative that you choose only materials and components that comply with safety regulations, but for collectors, traditional materials can be used.

# FABRICS

**Mohair** Mohair is the fleece of the Angora goat, woven into cotton backing then dyed and treated to create an enormous range of fabrics. It is possible to obtain mohair in almost any shade and with a range of different finishes that give a bear a specific look. The most common type has a straight pile in a variety of lengths from around 5mm to over 50mm. The shorter pile lengths are most suited to smaller bears. From this basic style, mohairs have been created that look worn or crushed, to make bears look older than they really are.

Distressed mohair has been treated to make the pile lie in random directions to give a bear a well-cuddled look.

Sparse mohair has far less pile woven into the backing to give the impression that much of the pile has worn away.

Tipped mohair, where the tip of the pile has been coloured to contrast with the pile underneath in either a darker or lighter shade, was very popular throughout the 1920s and is still available today.

There are many other styles available, including curly, wavy and embossed, which all add interest and texture to the pile.

**Synthetic fabrics** After World War II, alternative fabrics to mohair were actively sought. Man-made fibres were fully washable and made safe bears for children. Now there is an enormous range of synthetic fabrics available in a variety of qualities. Their main advantage is in their incredible range of colours. Natural 'fur' colours, from creams and golds to browns and black, are common as are some more outrageous colour schemes such as animal prints, rainbow stripes or ultra-bright lime green or orange!

At the cheapest end of the scale are the knitted-back fabrics that have a fairly thin pile. These are only suitable for making very softly stuffed toys as the backing will stretch out of shape when the toy is filled.

Middle range fabrics are of a much higher quality though they still have a knitted backing. The pile is far denser and the backing much firmer, reducing the stretching.

At the top of the range are very dense pile fabrics with a woven backing. These have a super-soft pile that makes stunning teddy bears. These fabrics are sometimes not as easy to find as the other qualities of synthetic fabrics and they can be more expensive than mohair.

For making smaller bears, 8–13cm (3–5in), there is a range of synthetic materials that make the process much easier. This special upholstery fabric has a backing that will not fray when sewn, which makes turning the pieces far easier. It is available in a wide choice of colours.

# PAD MATERIALS

**Felt** This was originally used for teddy bears' paws and pads and is still the most popular choice. As with most materials it is available in different grades, the most common being craft felt.

Craft felt is usually made from purely synthetic fibres and tends to be rather thin so if chosen it is best to use a double thickness.

A slightly higher quality felt has a large wool content in about a 60/40 mix. The natural fibre content gives the felt more durability and a thicker texture making it a perfect, low-cost material.

The best quality felt of all is made entirely from wool fibres. This material is very thick and hardwearing with a much finer texture than any other grade of felt.

**Leather and suede** Many old bears can be found with leather pads but these are usually just replacements on top of worn-out felt pads. Leather was rarely used on teddy bears but it can look very effective, although it can be a little difficult to sew. Hand-sewing the leather pads in place is probably the best way to achieve a neat and secure finish and for this a special leather needle and good strong thimble are essential!

**Ultrasuede** During the 1970s a new synthetic material was invented in the USA as an alternative to suede. This innovative fabric was soon incorporated into teddy bear design for use as a paw pad material as well as for making tiny miniature bears. The material, called Ultrasuede, is thin with a woven backing, which makes it very easy to sew and it is available in a good range of colours.

# FILLINGS

**Wood wool** This traditional filling is often mistaken for straw but is very finely shredded wood. It is still used today by teddy bear artists re-creating teddies of the past but is not suitable as a filling for a child's toy as it is not washable and has a high dust content. Wood wool is more time consuming to use than other fillings and needs to be packed in firmly and with care as it is easy to leave lumps and hollows which spoil the finished appearance.

**Kapok** This natural vegetable fibre was popular as a filling for teddy bears in the 1920s and 1930s. It was often used in conjunction with wood wool, which was used in the nose to aid embroidery and around growlers to stop them becoming clogged with the very fine kapok fibres. Although it is still used in the upholstery business today, kapok is no longer regarded as suitable for children's toys but teddy bear artists occasionally use it.

**Polyester** This is the most widely used filling material. It is easy to use, readily available and safe for children's toys. It is produced in different grades, the highest grade being the easiest to use as its silky texture and high bulk help make the stuffing process almost effortless. The slightly lower grade fillings are still easy to use though may compress more, leading to a lumpy finish.

**Pellets** During the 1980s and 1990s traditional teddy bear revival artists looked for new ways to add character to their designs and started using small plastic pellets along with polyester filling, to give the appearance of an old bear with filling that has collapsed over the years. Plastic pellets are the lightest and are best suited to larger bears. For smaller bears, tiny glass beads are used, smaller than plastic pellets and slightly heavier. Finally, for tiny bears, steel shot can be used. This is the smallest diameter pellet and is very heavy so, of course, is not recommended for larger teddies! Please do *not* be tempted to use lead shot in place of steel shot as it simply is not safe. Needless to say, any bear with pellets inside is not suitable for children.

# JOINTS

Traditional teddy bear joints have hardly changed over the whole century. In the beginning the large discs were made from cardboard or hardboard and the joints were attached with a large metal pin. Today, the joints are made in the same way using hardboard and are joined with a metal split pin. A few advances have been made though. Nuts and bolts can now be used to attach the joints, which are easier for bear-makers who have difficulty turning the metal pins. Wooden joints are not suitable for children's toys – for these, plastic joints should be used. These joints have evolved over the latter half of the teddy bear century due to safety considerations.

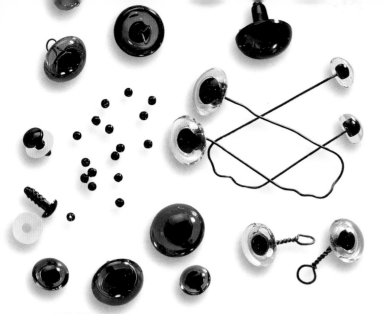

# EYES

**Boot buttons** The earliest teddies used boot buttons for eyes as they were plentiful at the time. Being round and black, they gave quite a good representation of an eye and were used for several years. Original boot buttons can still be obtained but it is more likely that you will find reproductions for use on bears.

**Glass eyes** Glass eyes, developed after 1909, had a stem of wire moulded into the back which, when looped, allowed the eye to be stitched into position. Initially just solid black, they were then made with pupils, with a clear glass surround often painted a realistic colour. Glass eyes today come in a wide variety of sizes and colours, some with enamelled backs making them very realistic.

**Safety eyes** In the 1960s, plastics were becoming commonplace and the safety aspect of children's toys had been realized. The pioneer of the safety eye for the teddy bear was Wendy Boston. This was a plastic eye fixed in position with rustproof nuts on the rear shank, making it secure and safe. The plastic safety eyes available today come in a huge range of colours and styles and can be substituted for glass eyes on any teddy bear.

**Position eyes** These eyes are absolutely fabulous and should be in every teddy bear-maker's workbox! They are black glass eyes that have sharp, pin-like wire on the back that enable you to try out a variety of eye sizes and positions before committing yourself to attaching your chosen eyes. They come in boxed sets in sizes 4–10mm and 11–16mm and will take the guesswork out of positioning eyes.

# NOSES

Most teddy bears have a hand-embroidered nose similar to the original teddy bear noses of the last 100 years. However, as with the safety eye, there is also a safety nose, which can be used instead. These noses are also made of plastic with a moulded shank at the rear on to which a non-removable washer is fitted to secure it in place. These noses can be very effective and can be covered with a complementary material to give a different look.

# VOICES

To give added realism to a bear, manufacturers fitted a 'voice box'. This was a simple weighted bellows system that forced air through a reed whenever the teddy bear was tipped either forward or back causing the teddy to give a throaty growl. Such mechanisms are still used although are usually encased in a plastic cylinder. Modern growlers are available in a choice of sizes and so can be fitted to almost any size bear.

# THREADS

**Sewing thread** For stitching your bear together on a sewing machine you will need to use a basic cotton thread in a colour that closely matches the fabric you are using.

**Strong thread** This thread is used in a variety of ways during the making of a teddy bear. If sewing your bear by hand, it is better to use strong thread rather than just basic cotton. It is also used to hand stitch the final closing seams and to attach glass eyes if they are being used.

**Nose thread** For teddy bears' embroidered noses you will need cotton perle thread in a suitable thickness and colour. The thinner thread is generally used for smaller bears but you may want to experiment with different thicknesses.

# TOOLS

When making teddy bears, there are a few basic tools that are needed, most of which will be found in the average household or are relatively inexpensive and easy to obtain.

**Templates and marking pens** To copy the patterns from this book, either photocopy them or trace them with tracing paper and a soft pencil. Paste these paper patterns on to lightweight card to make templates. Draw around the templates to transfer the pattern on to the back of the

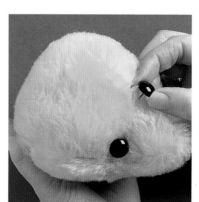

fabric. It is important to use a fine- or medium-tipped permanent marker pen for this as others may smudge and spoil the pile.

**Scissors** Use a general-purpose pair of scissors to cut out patterns and templates from paper and card. Good quality dressmaking scissors will be needed to cut out material with precision, essential when cutting mohair. Lastly, a small pair of embroidery scissors is useful for trimming thread ends and for final finishing touches to your bear such as trimming excess fur from the muzzle areas.

**Pins** As fur fabric is so thick, it is necessary to use extra long pins to hold the pieces together. It is also a good idea to use pins that have brightly coloured plastic or glass heads as these are easy to see and you will be far less likely to leave one in the bear.

**Needles** A range of different needles will be needed. If sewing a woven fabric, use a 'sharp' or regular point. For knitted-back fabrics use a ball-point needle. For hand sewing pieces use an ordinary 'sharp' needle in a size 5–7. When stitching final seams, a longer needle such as a 6.5cm (2½in) darning needle of about the same size, can be easier to use. This needle is also used for attaching ears but a curved needle could be used instead. Embroidering the nose will need a larger diameter needle – the size determined by the thickness of the nose thread. Finally, a very long needle is needed to attach glass eyes, long enough to pass right through the bear's head. These are usually sold as doll maker's needles and are available in sizes up to 18cm (7in) long.

**Thimble** Not everyone can sew using a thimble but it is a good idea to have one handy. During the various stages of making a bear, there are times when you may find it hard to pass the needle through the fabric and a thimble becomes invaluable. If you choose a leather thimble you can use it to protect your fingers when you have to pull strong thread tightly to secure seams.

**Pliers and cotter keys** A good quality pair of small, long-nosed pliers about 15cm (6in) will be needed for turning the split pins on traditional wooden joints. Cotter keys are shaped like a screwdriver with a slot in the end to turn the split pin, useful if you have trouble turning the pins with ordinary pliers.

**Awl** This is a sharp, pointed tool used to make small holes in cardboard templates and in fabric at the joint and eye positions. A small knitting needle would do instead.

**Stuffing sticks** You can buy stuffing tools to help fill your bear. These can be useful and are easy to use but are not essential – the handle of a wooden spoon and a chopstick are as effective.

**Teasel brush** When you have finished your bear you may find that some of the fur pile is trapped in the seams. A teasel brush, a simple block of wood with small wire bristles attached, is excellent at lifting the pile from seams and for general grooming. Similar brushes can be found in pet shops where they are sold as grooming brushes for small dogs.

# Step-by-step guide to

# Making a Traditional Teddy Bear

This section is a succinct guide to making a traditional teddy bear and is intended to be followed for all the bears in this book. Some techniques specific to the individual bears, such as inserting a growler or embroidering claws, are described in the bear chapters.

All the bear patterns can be found on pages 73–115. A seam allowance of 6mm (¼in) has been included in each pattern.

We recommend that if you choose to sew your bear on a sewing machine, each seam should be stitched twice for strength and durability. If you prefer to sew entirely by hand, follow the instructions for hand sewing techniques shown on the three miniature bears on page 71. Make sure to remove all pins as you go.

# Marking Fabric

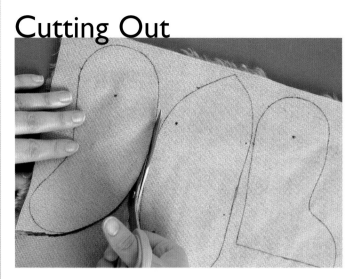

1 First, transfer your chosen pattern on to card to make a set of templates. Photocopy or trace the pattern pieces on to paper then glue them on to thin card and carefully cut out along the outline with scissors. Make holes in the templates with an awl for all important information, such as joint positions and openings as these will need to be transferred to the back of the fabric later. Make templates for all pieces that need to be reversed as well so that you cannot make a mistake when marking out.

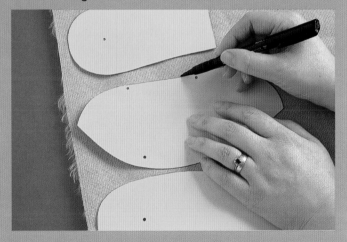

2 Find the direction of the pile on your fabric by brushing the fur with your hand – the smoothest way is the pile direction. Mark this with an arrow on the back of the fabric to use as a guide. On some materials, like distressed mohair, the pile goes in different direction, so check carefully. Lay all of the templates on to the back of the fabric as close together as you can, making sure that the arrows on the pattern pieces are all facing the same way as the arrow you marked on the fabric. With a fine, permanent marker, carefully draw around each piece and transfer all of the other important markings, such as joint and dart positions, at the same time.

# Cutting Out

1 When you have transferred all of the pattern pieces to the back of the fabric, carefully cut out each piece along the outline. Care must be taken when cutting fabrics with a pile as you only want to cut the backing fabric and not the fur. To ensure that you are cutting only the backing, slid the point of the bottom blade of your scissors through the pile to the backing and just slowly and carefully snip the fabric. Use small embroidery scissors on difficult or small pieces.

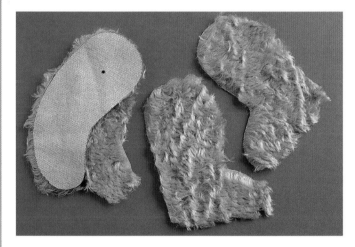

2 When you have cut out all of the pieces it is worthwhile taking a little time to pair up each of the pieces with its corresponding part to make sure that you have not inadvertently cut out two left arms (it can easily happen). Finally, transfer the paws and foot pads to your pad material in the same way, remembering that if you are using felt there is no grain direction to worry about so you can lay the pieces on to the fabric in the most economical way possible.

# Sewing the Head Sides

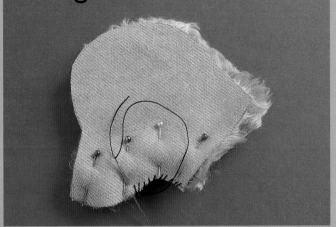

**1** The head is made up of two sides pieces and a gusset. Begin by placing the head side pieces fur sides together and pin along the 'under-chin' seam from points A to B, shown on the patterns. Over-sew the edges together to hold in position and stop the pieces moving about whilst sewing.

**2** Remove the pins and stitch the pieces together along this seam. To avoid too much fur becoming trapped in the seam, remove the oversewing stitches and use a teasel brush to brush along the seam from the wrong side to free the pile. It is best to do this carefully or the backing fabric may start to fray.

# Sewing the Head Gusset

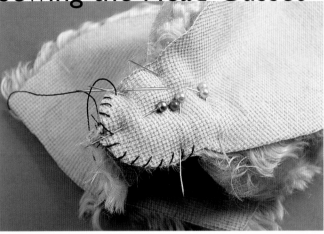

**1** The head gusset gives the head its three-dimensional shape. Pin the head gusset to the head sides at the nose first, matching point A. Next match point C on both sides of the head and pin to secure. Before you continue to pin the rest of the gusset in place, over-sew this section to hold it securely.

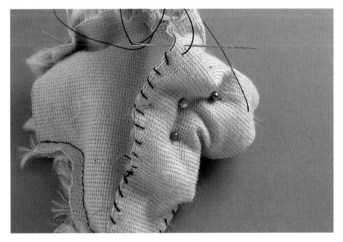

**2** Match points D on both sides of the head and pin in place then continue to pin the gusset to the head sides until it is firmly held together. Over-sew the edges together then stitch carefully in place. As the fabric is rather bulky, you may find it easier to sew the head gusset in by hand until you gain more experience. When complete, ensure all the fabric has been caught, remove all pins and tacking (basting) and turn the head right side out.

# Two-Piece Body

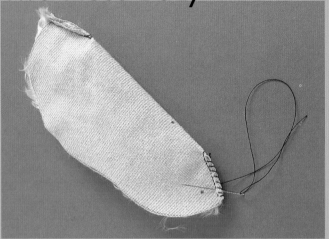

**1** Some bear designs have a body consisting of two pieces only, either with or without darts for added shape. To stitch darts, fold the body piece fur sides together so that the two edges of the dart at the top of the body meet. Over-sew together then stitch in place. Continue to make the other darts in the same way.

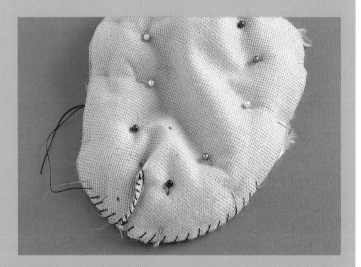

**2** After you have stitched all the darts, or if the design does not have them, place the two body pieces fur sides together. Match the seams of the darts at the top and bottom of the body and pin at these points. Over-sew in place, remembering to leave the opening as marked on the pattern clear, then stitch together. Brush out the seams with a teasel brush then turn right side out.

# Four-Piece Body

**1** Some designs consist of a body made up of four pieces. Place one body front piece on to a body back piece with fur sides together and matching points E, F and G. Pin along this edge only then over-sew and stitch in position. Brush out the seam with a teasel brush. Do exactly the same with the other body front and back pieces.

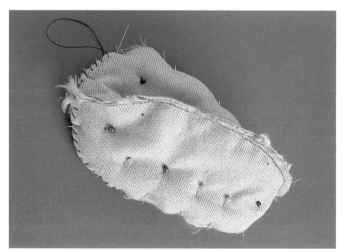

**2** Place the two partly completed body pieces fur sides together – points E and G should match up. Pin the pieces together around the entire edge and over-sew together, remembering to leave the opening as marked on the pattern, then stitch in place. It is important to finish off start and finish points securely as this opening is used for turning, jointing and stuffing. Brush out the seams then turn right side out.

# Sewing the Paw Pads

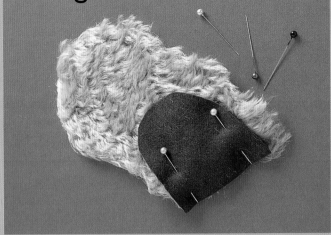

I Take one of the paw pad pieces and place it on top of one of the inner arm pieces, with right sides together so that the straight edges and points H and I match.

2 Pin the paw pad in place, tucking the fur pile in with the point of the pin as you go. Over-sew the pieces together along the straight edge then stitch the paw pad in place. Repeat with the other inner arm and paw pad.

# Sewing the Arms

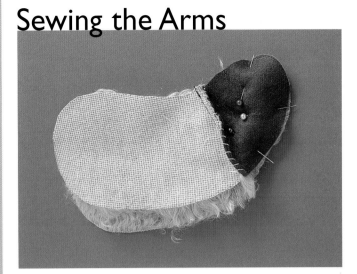

I Place one of the completed inner arms on to the corresponding outer arm piece, fur sides together. Place a pin at the top of the arm and another at the paw pad to hold in place. Continue to pin the arm pieces together, making sure that the fabric is not being stretched – if you find that it is not fitting together well, un-pin the arm and start again.

2 With the arm pinned securely, over-sew the edges together, leaving the opening for turning as marked on the pattern, then stitch in place.

# Sewing the Legs

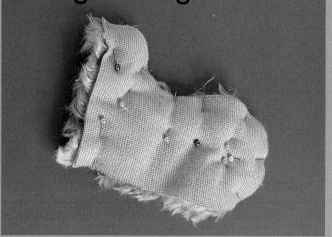

**1** Take two of the leg pieces and place them fur sides together, matching points J and K and keeping the bottom straight edge level. Pin all around the curved edges leaving the bottom straight edge open – this is for the foot pad, which will be inserted later.

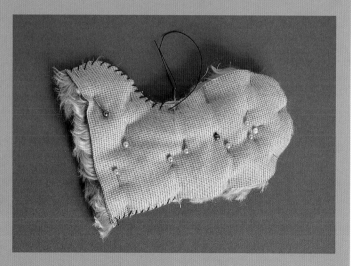

**2** Now over-sew the edges and stitch the leg pieces together. Remember to leave un-stitched the bottom straight edge and the opening, as marked on the pattern.

# Sewing the Foot Pads

**1** To make sure that the foot pad is inserted symmetrically, first take one of the felt pads and fold it in half along its length, creasing it as much as you can. This crease is the centre line of the foot pad. Starting at the toe (J), match the crease in the foot pad to the seam on the leg and pin in place. Do the same at the other end of the foot pad, matching the crease to the other seam on the leg (K). Continue to pin around the curved edges until the foot pad is held in place.

**2** Carefully over-sew the foot pad in position then stitch in place. As the appearance of the feet on bears is so important, it is a good idea to hand sew them in place so that they are perfectly symmetrical when finished. Repeat with the other leg then turn both legs right sides out.

# Limb Joints and Stuffing

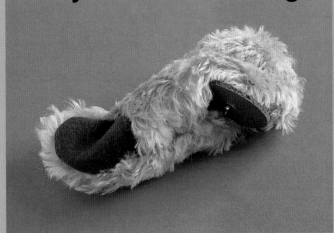

I Before you can begin stuffing the limbs, the joints have to be inserted. Take one split pin and thread on one metal washer followed by a wooden disc (this is a half-joint). Take a completed arm and, on the inside, find the mark that indicates the joint position. With an awl, make a small hole in the fabric, ready to pass the split pin through. Place the joint inside the arm, pushing the split pin through the hole to emerge on the outside. Place joints inside all four limbs in this way, making sure that you make both a left and right leg!

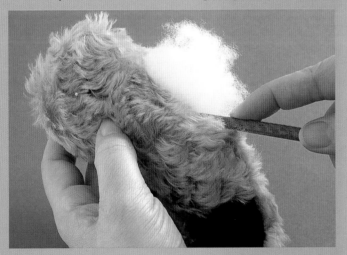

2 With the joints in position, the limbs can now be stuffed. Use as much stuffing as you reasonably can at one time to fill the limbs. Using tiny amounts will lead to a lumpy finish with lots of small air pockets. Fill the hardest-to-reach areas first, such as the pads, using stuffing sticks or a chopstick to help push it in firmly. If lumps start to appear, take the stuffing out and start again. Try to lay the stuffing in a lengthways direction to help give more rigidity to the limb.

# Closing Seams

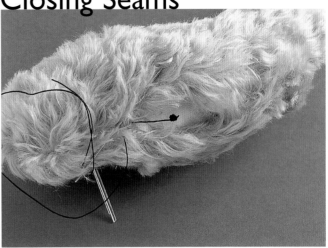

I Having stuffed all of the limbs, the final seams now have to be closed. This is done with a ladder stitch, which is a neat and invisible method of finishing. Thread a needle with extra strong thread and make a big knot at the end. At the top of the opening, pass the needle through the fabric from the inside so that the knot is invisibly anchored.

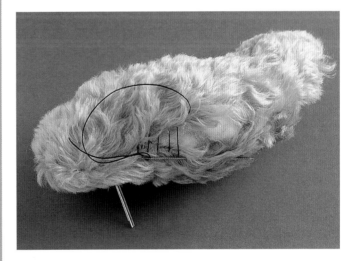

2 On the other side of the opening, directly opposite where the thread is anchored, make one small stitch so that the thread is bridging the gap between the two edges of the opening. The next small stitch is made directly opposite this stitch on the other side of the opening. Continue in this way, pulling the stitching as you proceed to close the seam, until you reach the bottom of the opening, where you can finish off the thread securely with a couple of small knots.

# Head Stuffing and Jointing

**1** The head is stuffed in much the same way as the limbs, the only difference being that the joint can only be inserted *after* the head has been filled. Check the head carefully after stuffing to make sure that the filling is evenly distributed and that the head looks 'balanced'. Take a half-joint and place the wooden disc on to the filling in the neck edge of the head with the split pin pointing outwards.

**2** Thread a needle with extra strong thread and stitch a large running stitch all around the neck edge of the head. Pull the thread tightly so that the fabric gathers over the wooden disc and around the split pin. This must now be finished off securely, so take lots of large stitches, passing from one side of the split pin to the other, then finish off the thread. It does not matter if it looks untidy as this will be hidden.

# Sewing the Ears

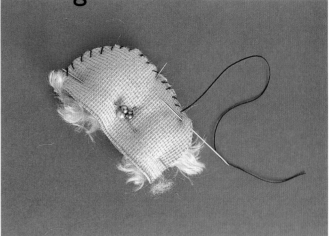

**1** Place two of the ear pieces fur sides together and pin around the curved edge, tucking in as much of the fur as you can. Over-sew the edges together, leaving the bottom straight edge open. Remove the pins and stitch around the curved edge only.

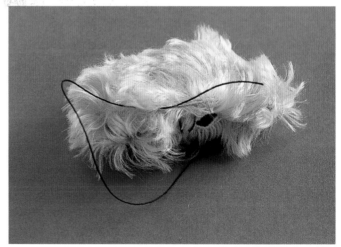

**2** Turn the ear right side out. Using a pin to help, tuck the raw edges along the bottom straight edge to the inside. Thread a needle with extra strong thread and close this seam with ladder stitch in the same way as closing the final seam on a limb (page 25). Repeat with the other ear pieces.

# Attaching the Ears

1 With both ears complete, they can now be attached to the head. Using the photograph of your chosen bear design as a reference, pin the ears in position on to the head. Try different positions to give your bear an alternative expression if you wish. Check that both ears are level and look symmetrically placed on the head.

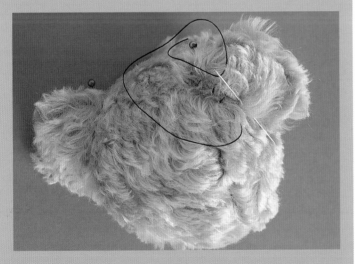

2 When you are happy with the placement of the ears, thread a needle with extra strong thread and knot the end. Start the thread at the back of the ear so that the knot will be invisible, then stitch the ears to the head using ladder stitch. As you progress, check that you are still happy with the way the ears look.

# Positioning the Eyes

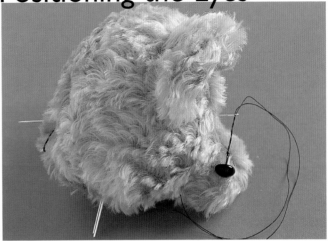

1 Use 'position eyes' to decide where you would like the eyes to be (see page 16). Experiment with placement and size to achieve a look that you are happy with. When you have decided what size you are going to use, attach a long length of extra strong thread very securely to the loop of each eye. Carefully remove one of the eyes and make a hole in the fabric with an awl. Thread one eye on to a long needle and pass the needle through the hole to emerge at the centre back of the head as near to the joint as you can. Repeat with the other eye, emerging about 2cm (¾in) away from the first eye.

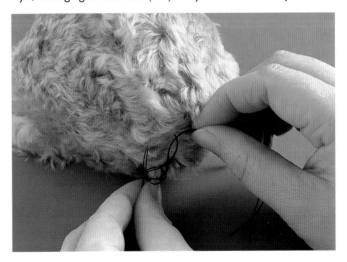

2 To hold the eyes in place, the threads are knotted together. Pull the threads as tightly as you can so that the eyes are pulled in and create natural sockets. It is easier if someone helps you by gently pushing on the eyes whilst you knot them at the back. Make three or four knots to be sure that the eyes will not come out.

# Nose Template

I If the thought of embroidering a nose seems a little daunting, here is a foolproof way of making sure it will turn out perfectly. Cut a nose shape from a scrap of felt or Ultrasuede in the same colour as the nose thread you are going to use. Try out different sizes and shapes, as this will affect how your bear will look. Pin the template temporarily in position. Use small embroidery scissors to trim away the fur pile from directly underneath the template, right down to the fabric backing.

2 Apply a thin layer of fabric glue to the felt template, then stick the template in place, making sure it is level and exactly where you want it. Leave to dry thoroughly before going on to embroider the nose.

# Stitching Nose and Mouth

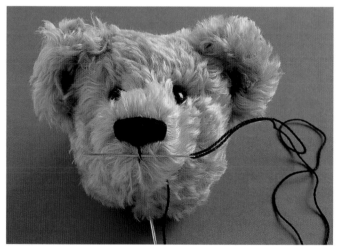

I Starting with a long length of nose thread, secure the end invisibly by taking a few stitches behind the template. Make a long straight stitch down the middle of the template, extending below the bottom edge of it. Start to work parallel stitches close together from the centre out to one edge, using the template as a guide. When you reach the edge, return to the centre and continue out to the other edge.

2 When the nose template is completely covered, bring the needle out at the point where the mouth will be. Pass the needle under the long central nose stitch, then insert it directly opposite the point it emerged, to create a symmetrical mouth. Check that it is level before you finish off the thread securely in the same way as you started.

# Final Assembly

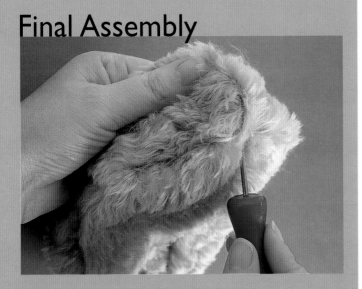

I Always start assembling your bear by attaching the head first. From the inside of the body find the marks that represent the joint positions. Using an awl, make a hole for the head joint. Pass the split pin of the head joint through this hole and, from the inside of the body, thread on another wooden disc followed by a metal washer.

2 Using pliers or a cotter key, turn down one of the legs of the split pin into a coil so that it sits on the washer. Repeat this action with the other leg of the pin, making sure that the joint is nice and tight. Attach the arms and legs in the same way, making sure that they are facing the correct way before securing the joint.

# Finishing and Grooming

I Now that all of the limbs are attached, all that remains is to fill the body cavity. You can use polyester to fill the body in the same way as the limbs but filling the cavity with beads can give your bear more character (see Fillings, page 15). Place a little polyester filling in the neck area of the body to support the head then fill the cavity with as many or few beads as you like. Fewer beads will give the impression of an old bear who's filling has collapsed. Place a small amount of polyester under the opening before closing the final seam with ladder stitch.

2 To make your bear look his best, give him a brush all over with a teasel brush. This will free any fur that is still trapped in the seams as well as lift the pile. Be very careful around the eyes, nose and felt pads, as the wire bristles will easily damage these areas.

# The Bears

## 1900s

## 1920s

## 1940s

## 1910s

## 1930s

## 1960s

## 1980s

## 1950s

## 1970s

## 1990s

# Albert

## A First Decade Bear

The very beginning of the twentieth century saw the development of a new toy that would become a lifelong companion to many children and prove to be one of the most enduring toys of all time. Bears of this first decade were fully jointed, imitating as closely as possible their real life counterparts, with humps on the back, large feet and long-snout noses. Some of the early designs were so realistic that they did indeed look rather fierce! Materials evolved quickly at this time and the need to find a realistic-looking fur was pioneered in Germany with the development of mohair fur fabric. Mohair was found to be the best material and is still used today for making the definitive teddy bear.

*From the very beginning, teddy bears were designed to look like real bears. Mohair was chosen as it closely resembled real fur and was easy to dye into natural 'bear-like' colours. Albert has been designed following these criteria with the addition of a centre seam on his head, which is now a sought-after feature on old bears from this era.*

# Albert 40cm (15¾in)

As the very early designs of teddy bears were intended to make them as realistic as possible, we have designed Albert with a humped back, long-snout nose, large feet and long arms. We have used cinnamon-coloured, sparse mohair to give Albert the appearance of a well-loved teddy bear of the period. We have also used replica shoe button eyes, as glass eyes were not introduced until a little later on. Again, to emulate real bears, the muzzle area has been shaved to reveal the fabric backing. One famous German manufacturer, when cutting out their pattern pieces, found that a head gusset could be made from two pieces sewn together making a centre seam, which maximized the use of the fabric available. This feature is reproduced in Albert and helps to re-create a teddy bear of the 1900–09 period.

## You will need

- 50 x 137cm (20 x 54in) of 15mm (⅝in) 'sparse' pile, cinnamon mohair

- 20 x 25cm (8 x 10in) wool felt for paws and pads

- Two x 50mm (2in) traditional wooden joints for the arms

- Three x 65mm (2½in) traditional wooden joints for the head and legs

- One pair 12mm (½in) matt black glass eyes on loops

- 3m (3¼yd) black perle cotton nose thread

- 500g (20oz) wood wool stuffing (or polyester stuffing)

- Sewing thread (to match fabric)

- Strong thread (to match fabric)

## Making Albert

This bear is made in the same way as described in the step-by-step guide on pages 19–29 and using the patterns on pages 74–77, with the exception of the head gusset, which is explained opposite. Wood wool stuffing was used from the beginning of bear design but it can be a little difficult to use as it tends to form itself into dense lumps, so if you prefer you can substitute polyester stuffing instead. Filling teddy bears with wood wool was considered a skilled job in the early days and this task was often left to the men!

A teddy bear collector is known as an arctophile, derived from two Greek words, *arcos* for bear and *philos* for love.

# Inserting a centre seam head gusset

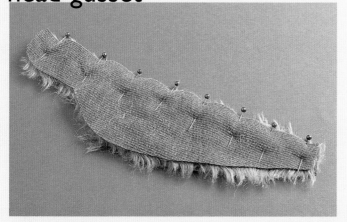

1 Place the two head gusset pieces fur sides together and securely pin along the straight edge.

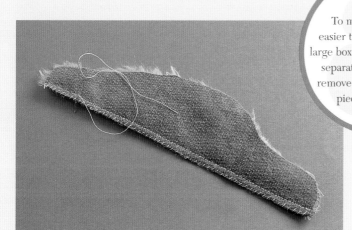

2 Over-sew the pieces together along the straight edge to prevent them from slipping, then stitch together.

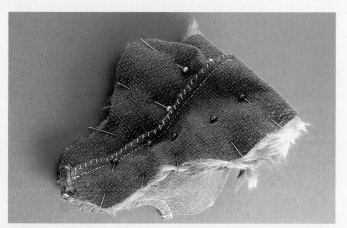

3 Insert the head gusset as described in the step-by-step guide on page 21, matching the seam on the head gusset with the seam on the head.

*During a particularly cold winter in 1906, Steiff produced a teddy bear hot-water bottle. Only ninety were ever made and surviving examples are very valuable.*

**Tip**
To make wood wool easier to use, place it in a large box, then tease it out to separate the strands and remove any large or sharp pieces before you begin.

*During this first decade nearly 400 songs were registered with the words 'Teddy' or 'Teddy Bear' in the title.*

# Frederick

## A Second Decade Bear

The popularity of teddy bears continued to grow enormously during the second decade, with the Steiff company expanding throughout Europe and into America and Australia. Greater competition encouraged companies to create different styles of bears and novelty designs were introduced, such as a bear on all fours attached to a wheeled chassis. Unusual colours of mohair were used to make bears for specific markets, such as black bears by Steiff, which were to be sold in Britain only. Up until this time boot button eyes were still commonly used but this decade saw the introduction of glass eyes, which gave a different look to teddy bears as the eyes could be made in different colours, such as blue with a black pupil. The outbreak of World War I halted trade throughout Europe, so many new British bear manufacturing companies became established, including Deans and Chad Valley.

*During this decade of teddy bear manufacture, designers still favoured realistic designs. Some manufacturers were so keen to make their bears appear real that they often ended up looking very fierce at the same time! You'll be happy to know that Frederick isn't at all fierce but he has been designed to resemble the realistic bears that were produced during the second decade.*

# Frederick 48cm (19in)

Although teddy bear design was moving forward at an incredible rate, the majority of designs still concentrated on teddy bears with a realistic look to them. Frederick is quite a large bear standing 48cm (19in) tall, so we have chosen to use beautiful long, curly pile mohair in a natural golden brown shade. Many teddy bears of this era had representative claws embroidered on to the paws and feet with black or brown thread so we have re-created this feature on Frederick. Manufacturers all had their own styles of embroidery for the claws and it is possible to identify some bears just by this feature. If a particular company inspires you it is easy to embroider the claws in their style if you wish.

## You will need

- 60 x 137cm (24 x 54in) of 25mm (1in) curly pile, golden brown mohair
- 20 x 25cm (8 x 10in) wool felt for paws and pads
- Two x 75mm (3in) traditional wooden joints for the legs
- Three x 65mm (2½in) traditional wooden joints for the head and arms
- One pair 16mm (⅝in) matt black glass eyes on loops
- 5m (5½yd) black perle cotton nose thread
- 800g (28oz) wood wool stuffing (or polyester stuffing)
- Sewing thread (to match fabric)
- Strong thread (to match fabric)

## Making Frederick

Although quite a large design, Frederick is made in the same way as described in the step-by-step guide on pages 19–29, and using the patterns on pages 78–84. For added realism, many old bears had claws embroidered on to their paws and feet, a feature that we have re-created on Frederick. This procedure, described opposite, is very easy and can be used on any bear design of any size.

The first comic strip bear to appear in a British newspaper was 'Bobby Bear' who appeared in 1919 in the *Daily Herald*.

# Embroidering claws

1 Decide how many claws you are going to have (we had four) then thread a long needle with perle nose thread and secure the end in the same way as for embroidering the nose on page 28.

2 Bring the needle out in the position of the first claw, close to or on the pad, then make one long stitch back into the fur. Now bring the needle out in the position of the second claw.

3 Continue in this way until all of the claws have been worked then finish off the thread securely in the same way as you started.

*A tiny Gebrüder Bing bear survived the sinking of the Titanic in 1912 and was returned to the family of its owner, who, sadly had not survived the disaster.*

## Tip

If you are using a long pile mohair you might like to trim the fur on the pads so that you can see the claws more clearly.

*Despite a cool reception to their first teddy bear design in 1902, by this decade Steiff had sold well over one million bears world-wide.*

# Percy

## A Third Decade Bear

The 1920s saw new innovations in teddy bear design. After the end of World War I there was a shortage of materials for making teddy bears, so manufacturers had to find other resources, such as reconstituted nettle plant in place of plush. However, by the end of the decade they were able to be more innovative again, developing new ideas and materials, such as a new 'tipped' fabric which proved to be very popular. Brushing the very tips of the pile with a darker shade of dye created this unusual look and original bears made from this fabric can sell for a great deal of money, such as 'Happy Bear', a 1920s Steiff example, which was sold at auction in 1989 for £55,000. In addition, kapok became the new filling for quality bears and was soon used by almost all bear manufacturers, as it was both hygienic and lightweight.

*By the 1920s, teddy bears had proved to be so popular that new ideas were embraced and became popular, such as 'tipped' mohair, where one shade of mohair has another colour applied to just the tips of the pile. Percy has been made with just such a tipped mohair.*

# Percy 39cm (15½in)

Percy is our interpretation of a teddy bear from the 1920s. He is 39cm (15½in) tall and we have made him from one of the many wonderful tipped furs that are available today and which are very similar to the 1920s originals. Percy's fur has a beige base with a dark brown tip and his muzzle has been trimmed to show the effect of the tipped mohair to full advantage. He has been filled with kapok stuffing, as many bears of that time would have been. By this time, glass eyes were in common use, having first been offered via Steiff catalogues in 1908. Percy is also able to give a reassuring growl, thanks to a growler inserted in his tummy. Growlers or voice boxes were very popular during this period, though they had first been introduced a decade earlier.

## You will need

- 50 x 137cm (20 x 54in) of 16mm (⅝in) tipped pile German mohair

- 15 x 25cm (6 x 10in) felt for paws and pads

- Five x 50mm (2in) traditional wooden joints

- One pair 16mm (⅝in) black glass eyes on loops

- 3m (3¼yd) brown perle cotton thread for nose

- 500g (20oz) kapok stuffing (or polyester stuffing)

- One medium-size growler

- Sewing thread (to match fabric)

- Strong thread (to match fabric)

## Making Percy

This bear is made by following the instructions in the step-by-step guide on pages 19–29 and using the patterns provided on pages 85–88. If you are working with kapok stuffing it is a good idea to wear a dust mask, as the very fine fibres can be irritating. Before filling the body cavity, you need to decide whether you would like to give your finished bear a 'voice'. Growlers are easy to insert and really animate the teddy – see illustrated instructions opposite.

A collection of teddy bears is known as a 'hug'.

# Inserting a growler

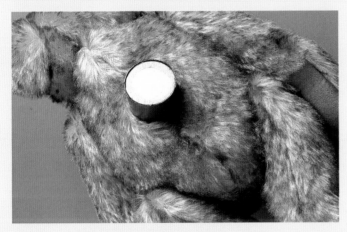

**1** Fill the body cavity to about three-quarters full, leaving a hollow large enough to take the growler.

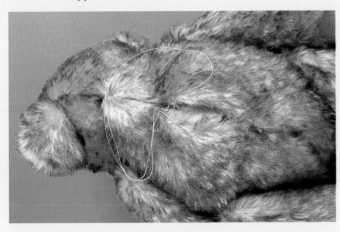

**2** Place the growler into the hollow with the holes on the top of the growler facing towards the bear's tummy. Placing it in this position will make the bear growl when he is tipped backwards.

**3** Make sure that the hard edges of the growler cannot be felt from the front, using more filling if necessary, then add more stuffing to cover it completely, making sure it is well padded. Close the final back seam with ladder stitch (see page 25).

*The soft stuffing often used in teddy bears was kapok, which was collected from the seed pods of the tropical tree Ceiba pentandra. Kapok was commonly used in the manufacture of life-jackets.*

## Tip

To make the bear growl when tipped forwards, place the growler with the holes facing the open back seam.

*Mohair is the fleece of the angora goat, which is woven into cotton backing and then dyed and treated to create an enormous range of fabrics.*

# Clarence

## A Fourth Decade Bear

This decade saw no halt to the popularity of teddy bears and more manufacturers became established to feed the demand for the toys. Merrythought Ltd was established in Shropshire, England and made traditional bears as well as novelty designs. The realistic design of teddy bears produced in the previous decades, with their long noses and long limbs, was dropped in favour of more friendly looking bears, although shorter, shaved muzzles were still favoured. Manufacturing methods were simplified and where possible fabric pieces were cut out in one piece and then folded ready for sewing together. The start of World War II changed teddy bears and the way they were designed, as materials and demand became scarce.

*Teddy bears had well and truly established themselves in the toy market by the 1930s and manufacturers started to develop their own unique styles. Cutting the pattern pieces in one so that they were folded, saved time during manufacture as well as making economic use of materials. Clarence is made in this way and is a very easy and quick bear to make.*

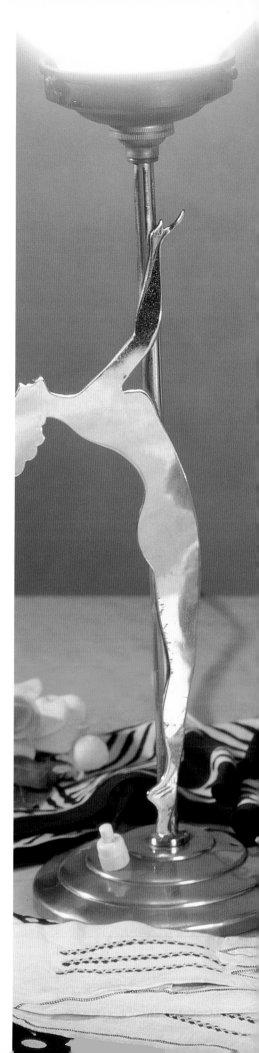

# Clarence  40cm (15¾in)

Our version of a 1930s teddy is Clarence, a 40cm (15¾in) tall bear made from a natural light brown mohair. As with many designs of this era, Clarence has shorter limbs and small, rounder feet than his ancestors but the ears remain large. He is simple to make as the arm and leg pieces can be folded together and stitched, a method of working that makes the bear quick and easy to sew. A small area on his muzzle has been trimmed down to the backing fabric, like many bears during the 1930s. As kapok was still the filling of choice for most bears we have opted to use this but as it can prove difficult to embroider the nose when the head is filled with kapok, we also added a little wood wool just in the muzzle area.

## You will need

- 50 x 137cm (20 x 54in) of 15mm (⅝in) embossed pile, light brown mohair
- 15 x 15cm (6 x 6in) upholstery velvet for paws and pads
- Two x 50mm (2in) traditional wooden joints for the arms
- Three x 65mm (2½in) traditional wooden joints for the head and legs
- One pair 12mm (½in) amber glass eyes on loops
- 3m (3¼yd) black perle cotton nose thread
- 500g (20oz) kapok stuffing (or polyester stuffing)
- Small amount of wood wool
- Sewing thread (to match fabric)
- Strong thread (to match fabric)

## Making Clarence

This bear has been designed slightly differently to the other teddy bears in the book as the inner and outer arms are cut in one piece, as are the legs. The pieces are folded before sewing them together, which was a method used in the 1930s to speed up manufacture. This is only a slight difference to the design and the rest of the bear can be made in the same way as described in the step-by-step guide on pages 19–29, and using the patterns on pages 89–93.

It has been estimated that forty per cent of adults still own their childhood teddy bear.

# Making folded arms and legs

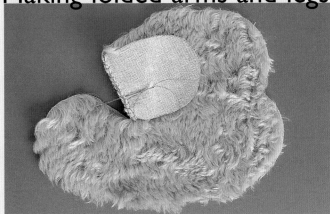

**1** Place the paw pad on the inner arm side with right sides together and matching the straight edge. Over-sew to hold in position then stitch in place.

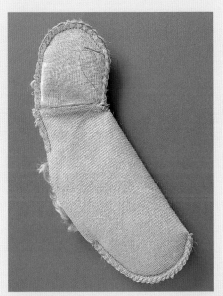

**2** Fold the arm in half with fur sides facing, pin and over-sew in position then stitch, remembering to leave the opening for turning as marked on the pattern.

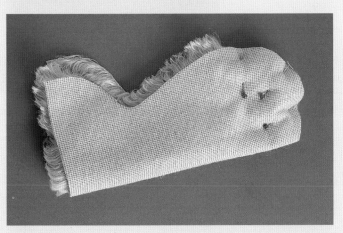

**3** For the legs, fold each leg piece in half and pin, over-sew then stitch in place, leaving the opening as marked on the pattern. The foot pad can then be inserted in the normal way (see page 24).

*After the coronation of George VI in 1936, many British manufacturers started producing patriotic teddy bears in red, white and blue.*

### Tip

When trimming muzzles, cut in the direction of the fur for a smooth, graduated look.

*In 1937, British Lines Bros, at this time the largest toy manufacturer in the world, launched its 'Pedigree' range of soft toys.*

# Douglas

## A Fifth Decade Bear

World War II brought many changes to the teddy bear industry but nevertheless the teddy was to prove one of the most comforting toys for children everywhere during these difficult times. Materials were in very short supply, which led to a dramatic change in the way bears were designed. As a cost-cutting measure they were made with much shorter limbs and with far less pronounced muzzles. Everything became more compact and alternative fabrics were sought – sheepskin was tried to good effect, as was artificial silk plush. To save on the more expensive plush fabrics, manufacturers designed teddies with 'sewn-on' clothes made from cheaper cotton-based fabrics which formed part of the body structure and therefore could not be removed.

*The austere World War II years forced manufacturers to redesign the teddy bear with the emphasis on economic use of available materials. This resulted in shorter arms and legs, smaller feet and less protruding muzzles. Douglas has been designed with these constraints to reflect the period, including the use of sparse mohair to give the impression of less sumptuous fabric.*

# Douglas 28cm (11in)

In line with the changes in teddy bear design during this decade, Douglas is a much smaller bear standing just 28cm (11in) tall, though he is still a toy to be proud of! For this design, we used toffee-coloured sparse pile mohair to emulate the cheaper, less sumptuous fabrics that would have been used throughout this period. Although the screw-in safety eye had been patented at the end of this decade, glass eyes were still more likely to be used so we have included these on Douglas. Rather than sew the ears on after the head has been filled and jointed, Douglas has his ears sewn into small slits cut into the side of the head. This is a traditional method of attaching ears for some manufacturers, whilst others preferred to add the ears at a later stage.

## You will need

- 25 x 137cm (10 x 54in) of 8mm (⅜in) sparse pile, toffee-coloured mohair
- 10 x 15cm (4 x 6in) wool felt for paws and pads
- One x 36mm (1½in) traditional wooden joint for the head
- Four x 25mm (1in) traditional wooden joints for the arms and legs
- One pair 8mm (⅜in) black glass eyes on loops
- 2m (2¼yd) black perle cotton nose thread
- 150g (5oz) kapok stuffing (or polyester stuffing)
- Sewing thread (to match fabric)
- Strong thread (to match fabric)

## Making Douglas This bear

is mainly made in the same way as described in the step-by-step guide on pages 19–29, using the patterns on pages 94–95; the only difference is in the way that the ears are attached to the head. The completed ears are sewn into slits that have been cut in the head pieces before the head is made in the normal way. This method of attaching ears (described opposite) is very secure and helps to prevent the ears being pulled off.

Teddy bears were in short supply during this decade as manufacturers world-wide turned to essential war work.

# Attaching ears in slits

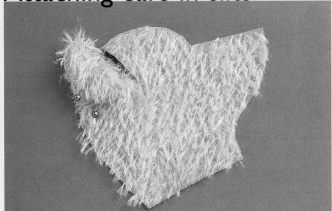

**1** Place a completed ear on to a head piece with fur sides together and the straight bottom edge of the ear lying along the edge of the slit. Pin in place. The ear will extend above the top of the head a little way.

**2** Fold the head piece over so that the nose is level with the back edge of the head and the ear is enclosed. Over-sew through all of the layers to hold in place, then stitch.

**3** Fold the top of the ear that extends above the head towards the front and over-sew the bottom of the ear to the head to hold in place. The head can now be made in the normal way.

*British manufacturers took advantage of the lack of foreign competition during the early years of the war, but as time progressed many smaller manufacturers were forced out of business.*

## Tip

If you prefer to attach the ears in the normal way, do not cut the slits in the head sides.

*As teddy bears became scarcer, magazines printed patterns for housewives to produce their own toys from salvaged materials.*

# Tommy

## A Sixth Decade Bear

The end of World War II did not bring an immediate end to shortages of materials. Synthetic plush became a popular fabric and even though many manufacturers were still using wood wool, polyester became the filling of choice. All-in-one, un-jointed, fully washable designs were introduced during this time. These bears were filled with foam rubber chips and made use of the new screw-on safety eye, making them ideal for young children. Once a manufacturer hit on a popular design it remained largely unchanged for many years, with the same bears being made in a variety of different sizes. During this period, traditional proportions were re-established but humped backs had largely disappeared. Complementary details such as embroidered claws, readily added to earlier bear designs, were often omitted to speed up manufacture.

*After the war years, the trend for big teddy bears was irresistible even though materials were still not readily available. Brighter coloured furs also helped to lift the spirits of the nation and encouraged the return to prosperity. Some of the larger teddies were manufactured to be able to stand up unaided. We have included these features in our design for Tommy.*

# Tommy

70cm (27½in)

Tommy re-creates a typically large bear from the 1950s, as 'big' was becoming beautiful. This bear was inspired by Brian's childhood teddy bear (also called Tommy!). Very large bears such as these often had the foot pads reinforced with card or hardboard, which enabled the bear to stand unaided. We have reproduced this feature in this design so this bear will really stand head and shoulders above the rest! By this time, teddy bears were available in all sorts of colours but as the traditional brown and gold shades continued to be the most popular, we have made Tommy from particularly stunning honey gold mohair. We have filled him with kapok, which was still in widespread use as was wood wool, often with the two fillings being used in different parts of the same bear depending on the manufacturer.

## You will need

- ◆ 100 x 137cm (40 x 54in) of 20mm (¾in) crushed long pile, honey gold mohair

- ◆ 30 x 25cm (12 x 10in) Ultrasuede for paws and pads

- ◆ Five x 90mm (3½in) traditional wooden joints

- ◆ One pair 16mm (⅝in) amber glass eyes on loops

- ◆ 3m (3¼yd) black perle cotton nose thread

- ◆ 2000g (70oz) kapok stuffing (or polyester stuffing)

- ◆ Sewing thread (to match fabric)

- ◆ Strong thread (to match fabric)

- ◆ Cardboard for pads

## Making Tommy

Tommy is a huge bear but he is made in exactly the same way as described in the step-by-step guide on pages 19–29 and using the patterns provided on pages 96–100 (the pattern pieces will need to be enlarged on a photocopier). As he is such a large bear, Tommy has had his foot pads reinforced with cardboard which has two benefits – the foot pads on large bears can tend to look too rounded so cardboard prevents this happening and also, with such nice flat feet, Tommy will be able to stand up all on his own.

Statistically, the teddy bear was still proving to be one of the most popular toys.

# Making reinforced pads

**I** Before stuffing the legs, cut a piece of card to shape using Tommy's foot pad template on page 100. This will need to be trimmed to fit inside the foot snugly.

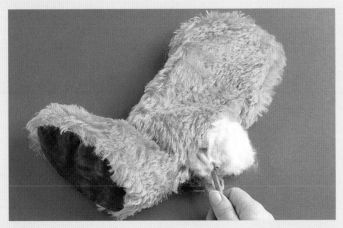

**2** Place the card inside the foot checking that it fits well with no puckers being formed in the foot or leg.

**3** The leg can now be stuffed in the normal way, taking care not to use undue force, which may bend and crease the card insert.

*Sooty, a teddy bear glove puppet, shot to fame on British children's television. He was created by Harry Corbett, a nephew of Harry Ramsden who was world famous for his chain of fish and chip shops.*

## Tip

If you prefer the feet to be of more rounded appearance then omit the card inserts and stuff in the normal way.

*Wood wool, which was commonly used for filling bears up until this time, was usually made from lime wood and was given the brand name of 'Excelsior'.*

# Carnaby

## A Seventh Decade Bear

By the 1960s children's toys had come under scrutiny and certain standards of manufacture had to be met. Wendy Boston's company pioneered fully washable, safe teddy bears that proved so popular the company was soon producing over a quarter of the UK's total soft toy exports. Strict guidelines were set and glass eyes were passed over in favour of safe plastic eyes, which could not be detached or gripped by fingers or teeth. The designs for child-safe teddy bears did not resemble traditional bears: often the arms and legs would be very short with no paw pads and the bear would be in a permanent sitting position with outstretched arms. Older, well-established firms still continued to make their traditional designs, having substituted components to comply with safety standards, so their bears were still fully jointed with moving head, arms and legs.

*During this decade, manufacturers had to conform to standardized safety standards for all soft toys both for durability and flammability. Fabrics had to be treated so that they became flame resistant and eyes had to be attached so that fingers or teeth couldn't grip them. Carnaby has been designed with safety in mind and is safe to be given to a child when made from the materials recommended here.*

# Carnaby 36cm (14in)

We have designed Carnaby to represent a traditional golden yellow teddy bear from the 1960s. He is perfectly suitable for a child as he is made using only safety components and is filled with polyester filling. Safety components are very easy to use and can be substituted with traditional joints if you are not making Carnaby for a young child. Gold mohair remained a very popular choice for a traditional teddy bear and many manufacturers reserved this colour for their best, top-of-the-range designs. Dark colours of synthetic fabrics were regularly chosen for the pads so we have re-created the style by using dark brown upholstery velvet, which gives a lovely contrast to the luxurious golden mohair fabric. When your bear is complete, don't forget to add a sumptuous satin ribbon of a nice bright colour that will complete the style of the period.

## You will need

- ◆ 40 x 137cm (16 x 54in) of 18mm (¾in) straight pile, gold mohair
- ◆ 15 x 20cm (6 x 8in) dark brown velvet for paws and pads
- ◆ Three x 50mm (2in) plastic safety joints for the legs and head
- ◆ Two x 36mm (1½in) plastic safety joints for the arms
- ◆ One pair 14mm (⁹⁄₁₆in) plastic amber safety eyes
- ◆ 2m (2¼yd) black perle cotton nose thread
- ◆ 350g (12oz) polyester stuffing
- ◆ Sewing thread (to match fabric)
- ◆ Strong thread (to match fabric)

## Making Carnaby

Follow the instructions in the step-by-step guide on pages 19–29 to make Carnaby, using the patterns on pages 101–103. The use of plastic safety joints and eyes make this bear a suitable toy for a child to play with but if you would rather use wooden joints, these can be substituted. Safety components can be used in any bear design without any radical change to the outward appearance.

In 1961 toy safety standards on flammability were announced by the British Standards Institution.

# Fitting safety eyes and joints

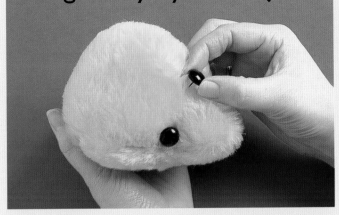

1 To position safety eyes accurately, first stuff the head so that you get a good idea of the finished shape. Use 'position eyes' to decide exactly where you would like the eyes to be placed and mark the spot lightly with a marker pen.

2 Remove the stuffing and make a hole at the marked position, large enough to take the shank of the eye. From the inside of the head, firmly push on the washer to hold the eye in place. The head can now be re-stuffed.

3 Attaching the head and limbs with safety joints is very similar to using wooden joints. Fit the joints inside the arms, legs and head in the same way as described on pages 25 and 26 for using wooden joints. From the inside of the body find the marks that indicate joint positions and make holes large enough to take the shanks. Pass the shank through the hole and firmly fix the washer in place.

*Cartoon teddy bears grew in popularity on television, with characters such as 'Yogi' bear, 'Winnie the Pooh' and 'Humphrey B. Bear'.*

**Tip**
Use a cotton reel as a tool to secure the washers for the safety eyes and joints firmly on to their shanks.

*During this decade manufacturers reviewed their methods as safety standards become more stringent.*

# Rowan

## An Eighth Decade Bear

By this decade teddy bears reached their peak as the world's most popular soft toy. The mass-produced designs that are available all over the world are largely made in factories based in the Far East. With more and more exciting toys for children to choose from, teddy bear manufacturers tried to keep their share of the market by creating cuter, more appealing bears that were completely different from the traditional types that had proved so popular over the years. Details were added such as stencilled paw markings on the feet, and airbrushing was used to enhance other areas such as the eyes and ears, which added greatly to the teddy bear's character. Many traditional teddy bear manufacturers ceased trading at this time but a new craze for teddy bear collecting was about to sweep the world.

*To keep alive the interest in teddy bears, manufacturers felt the need to redesign the toy to be more appealing, with cuter features and softer fabrics. The colours of the various fabrics tended to differ from the traditional, natural colours so favoured up to this point. Rowan exhibits other popular ideas from this time – paw prints on his feet and a matching 'berry' red nose.*

# Rowan 36cm (14in)

Cute and cuddly was the order of the day for teddy bears during the 1970s and Rowan certainly lives up to that description! We have used long, straight pile mohair and polyester filling, which was used in almost all teddies of this era due to the strict safety standards now in force for soft toy manufacture. On his foot pads we have created an eye-catching paw print design. These simple shapes are cut from Ultrasuede and stuck on his feet. Ultrasuede, a new fabric from America, appeared in the 1970s. This material does not fray and is very simple to use without the need for hemming. To complete Rowan we have taken the same material and covered a plastic safety nose. This includes a little extra wadding to create a soft berry nose – hence this little bear's name of Rowan!

## You will need

- 40 x 137cm (16 x 54in) of 18mm (¾in) straight pile, natural mohair

- 15 x 20cm (6 x 8in) white Ultrasuede for paws and pads

- 10 x 15cm (4 x 6in) dark red Ultrasuede for nose and paw prints

- Five x 50mm (2in) plastic safety joints

- One pair 16mm (⅝in) black plastic safety eyes

- One 30mm (1³⁄₁₆in) plastic safety nose

- 400g (14oz) polyester stuffing

- Sewing thread (to match fabric)

- Strong thread (to match fabric)

- All-purpose craft glue

## Making Rowan

This cute bear is made using the patterns provided on pages 104–107, in the same way as described in the step-by-step guide on pages 19–29. Before you stuff the head you will have to fit the safety eyes (if using them) as well as the completed, padded safety nose – follow the instructions opposite. To attach the paw prints, use a good all-purpose glue suitable for fabrics.

The teddy bear is a popular marketing choice for charities.

# Paw prints and safety nose

I The paw prints are added to the bear's feet after they have been completed so that they can be placed symmetrically. First glue on the large pad followed by the centre two 'toes'. The final two 'toes' can be glued in place making sure that all of the pieces are symmetrically placed and the overall effect is well balanced.

2 To create a padded nose, run a large running stitch around the outside edge of the nose cover and pull gently so that it is slightly cupped. Place a small amount of polyester filling in the cover and lay the safety nose on top.

3 Pull the thread to gather the nose cover around the shank of the safety nose and finish off the thread securely. Check that the nose is well padded and smooth before you attach it to the head in the same way as attaching safety eyes (see Carnaby, page 59).

*The invention of the material Ultrasuede in the USA proved popular in teddy bear manufacture for paw pads.*

## Tip

The paw print can be stencilled on to the foot pad if you prefer, using a stencil brush and acrylic paint.

*The character teddy bear from books and television started to evolve as a variation on the traditional teddy bear.*

# Tia and Henry

## Ninth Decade Bears

A new fever gripped the world during the 1980s with teddy bear collecting being taken very seriously. Many books were published on their history and manufacture as the demand for information grew. Auction houses introduced teddy bear only sales as more and more old bears came up for sale, and it wasn't long before the £1000 barrier was broken when an early Steiff bear was sold at Sotheby's in London. Manufacturers saw an opportunity and started to produce replicas of their early designs in limited editions for collectors. Teddy bear artists emerged and began producing very high quality, handmade designs in very limited numbers, often with the addition of exquisite outfits and little bears of their own. As these bears were intended for the collectors' market, many artists used traditional materials such as glass eyes and wooden joints for authenticity.

*To take advantage of the renewed interest in the traditional teddy bear, teddy bear artists emerged focusing on attention to detail and individuality. Many of their bears are only available as limited editions or one-off designs. Leading manufacturers also recognized the interest and started reproducing old, original designs. Tia and Henry are typical examples of the kind of bear that design artists were producing.*

# Tia and Henry 34cm (13½in) & 16cm (6in)

Tia and Henry are characteristic of the type of bears that teddy bear artists were designing during the 1980s. We have used traditional materials throughout the designs, from top quality German mohair to the best grade of glass eyes on both Tia and Henry. Quality of materials and attention to detail are all-important factors to teddy bear artists and the addition of simple but well made outfits add greatly to a teddy bear's character. Tia is dressed in an easy-to-make pinafore dress and has a matching hair-band made from the same material. Henry is made to co-ordinate, with the very simple addition of a neck scarf and a small patch sewn on to his tummy.

## You will need for Tia

- ◆ 40 x 137cm (16 x 54in) of 15mm (⅝in) embossed pile, light brown mohair
- ◆ 15 x 20cm (6 x 8in) Ultrasuede for paws and pads
- ◆ Five x 36mm (1½in) traditional wooden joints
- ◆ One pair 14mm (⅝in) smokey topaz glass eyes on loops
- ◆ 3m (3¼yd) brown perle cotton nose thread
- ◆ 225g (8oz) polyester stuffing
- ◆ 50 x 112cm (20 x 44in) cotton print fabric
- ◆ Five x 12mm (½in) buttons
- ◆ Sewing thread (to match fabric)
- ◆ Strong thread (to match fabric)

## Making Tia and Henry

These delightful bears are made in the same way, as described in the step-by-step guide on pages 19–29. Patterns for both bears and Tia's dress are on pages 108–112. You will also need to cut out a rectangular skirt piece 60 x 14cm (24 x 5½in) and four strap pieces each 19 x 3.5cm (7½ x 1⅜in).

## You will need for Henry

- ◆ 25 x 40cm (10 x 16in) of 12mm (½in) sparse pile, chocolate mohair
- ◆ 10 x 10cm (4 x 4in) wool felt for paws and pads
- ◆ Three x 18mm (¾in) traditional wooden joints for head and legs
- ◆ Two x 12mm (½in) traditional wooden joints for arms
- ◆ One pair 4mm (³⁄₁₆in) black glass eyes on loops
- ◆ 1m (1yd) black perle cotton nose thread
- ◆ 110g (4oz) polyester stuffing
- ◆ Sewing thread (to match fabric)
- ◆ Strong thread (to match fabric)

# Making Tia's clothes

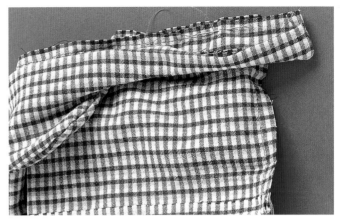

**1** Along the long edge of one of the bodice pieces, press the seam allowance to the wrong side to create a neat edge. Place the two bodice pieces right sides together and stitch all around, leaving the long straight edge open. Turn right side out and press. Hem the bottom edge and sew a large running stitch along the top edge of the skirt piece, then with right sides together, bring the two short sides together and stitch to within 4cm (1½in) of the top edge.

**Tip**

As Henry is such a small bear you may find it easier to sew him by hand. The technique for hand stitching can be found on page 71.

**2** Gather the top edge of the skirt so that it fits the bodice. With right sides together pin the raw straight edge of the bodice to the top of the skirt, allowing the bodice to extend beyond the skirt edge at the point marked on the pattern, on one side only. Stitch in place, and then bring the neatened edge over to enclose the seam and over-sew it in place.

**3** Make each pinafore strap by placing two strap pieces right sides together and stitching all around, leaving an opening for turning. Turn right side out, then neatly over-sew the opening closed. Press, then attach to the dress using buttons front and back. Add another button or press-stud to the back of the skirt. Finish with a length of fabric tied to make a bow for Tia and a scarf for Henry.

The term 'teddy bear artist' emerged to describe the makers of cottage industry, collectable bears.

# Honey, Pumpkin and Nutmeg

## Tenth Decade Bears

Across Europe more and more teddy bear artists became established, making bears in limited editions or exclusive designs for one outlet only. Internationally recognized awards were introduced in praise of their skill and achievements. With the interest in teddy bears so high, specialist magazines and books were published dedicated to all areas, including the history of teddy bears, information about manufacturers, and books of designs for readers to make their own bears, including our first title *Making Traditional Teddy Bears*. With more teddy bear artists emerging all over the world, designers had to find ways of making their bears stand out amongst the thousands of other bears competing for buyers' attention. Some artists allowed their imaginations to run riot whilst others took their inspiration from original teddy bear designs and made their own exquisite versions in miniature.

*In a new approach to teddy bear design, artists returned to making more traditional bears but still expressing individuality. The new miniature-bear artists impressed everyone with their precise skills, starting a new direction for the collector – one quickly taken on board by some of the larger manufacturers. Honey, Pumpkin and Nutmeg are traditional in design, made in a smaller scale to follow this new trend.*

# Honey, Pumpkin and Nutmeg 9cm (3in), 13cm (5in) & 13cm (5in)

With the introduction of miniature teddy bear making, a new collecting 'craze' began as many artists turned their attention to developing and perfecting the special skills needed to create such tiny works of art. Our three delightful miniature bears are based on very traditional designs from earlier in the century, albeit with a modern twist! Many of the materials we have used differ little to the type that would have been available many years ago, with the exception of the filling.

As miniature bears are so small they tend to be very lightweight so, to give them a more satisfying weight, we have used a contemporary filling, steel shot, in the tummies of the little bears. Steel shot is very heavy and a little placed in the body cavity can add a great deal of character to small bears.

## You will need for Honey

- 20 x 20cm (8 x 8in) of 5mm (³⁄₁₆in) pile, honey-coloured mohair

- 8 x 8cm (3½ x 3½in) wool felt for paws and pads

- Five x 10mm (⅜in) traditional wooden joints

- One pair 4mm (³⁄₁₆in) amber glass eyes on loops

- ½m (½yd) black perle cotton nose thread

- 15g (½oz) polyester stuffing

- 15g (½oz) steel shot

- Sewing thread (to match fabric)

- Strong thread (to match fabric)

## You will need for Pumpkin

- 25 x 25cm (10 x 10in) of 5mm (³⁄₁₆in) pile, pumpkin-coloured mohair

- 8 x 8cm (3½ x 3½in) wool felt for paws and pads

- Five x 12mm (½in) traditional wooden joints

- One pair 4mm (³⁄₁₆in) black glass eyes on loops

- ½m (½yd) black perle cotton nose thread

- 25g (1oz) polyester stuffing

- 25g (1oz) steel shot

- Sewing thread (to match fabric)

- Strong thread (to match fabric)

## You will need for Nutmeg

- 20 x 33cm (8 x 13in) of 12mm (½in) distressed pile, nutmeg-coloured mohair

- 8 x 8cm (3½ x 3½in) wool felt for paws and pads

- Five x 12mm (½in) traditional wooden joints

- One pair 4mm (³⁄₁₆in) black glass eyes on loops

- ½m (½yd) black perle cotton nose thread

- 50g (2oz) polyester stuffing

- 25g (1oz) steel shot

- Sewing thread (to match fabric)

- Strong thread (to match fabric)

# Hand sewing a bear

**1** Place the pieces fur sides together and pin to secure. Over-sew the edges together to stop the pieces from moving around, remembering to leave the opening as marked on the pattern.

## Making Honey, Pumpkin and Nutmeg
All three of these little bears are made from the patterns on pages 113, 114 and 115 and following the detailed instructions in the step-by-step guide on pages 19–29. The method of making small bears is exactly the same as for larger versions except that it is far more difficult to manoeuvre a sewing machine around tight curves, therefore it is better to sew small bears by hand following the illustrated instructions given here. See page 39 for instructions on embroidering claws.

### Tip
Try experimenting with other fillings, such as plastic pellets or glass beads in different sized bears.

**2** Sew the seams using an ordinary running stitch but keep your stitches as small as you can. When you have completed the seam, reverse the direction and fill in the gaps between the stitches for a good strong seam.

**3** Steel shot can be used to fill any part of the bear except the head. To use it in arms and legs, place a small amount of polyester filling to cover the paw pads so that they stay smooth. For the body, place a little polyester in the neck to support the head then add as much or little of the shot as you like to achieve the look you want.

*A world record price of £110,000 was paid for an old example of a Steiff bear, proving that teddy bears are here to stay!*

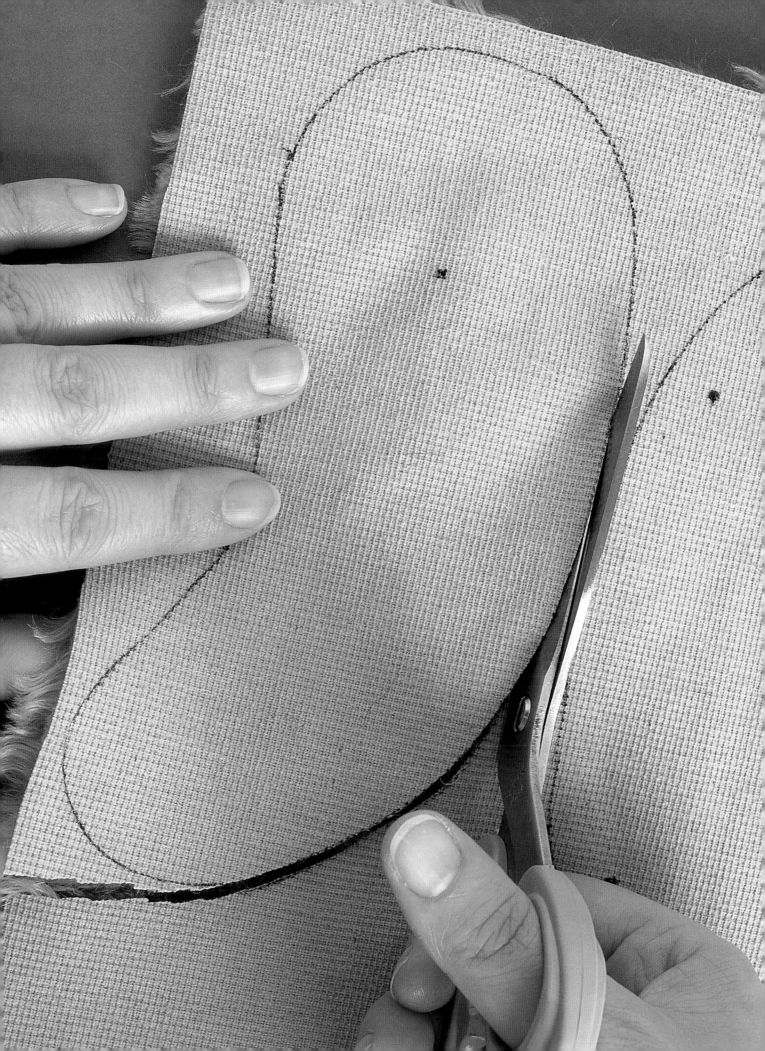

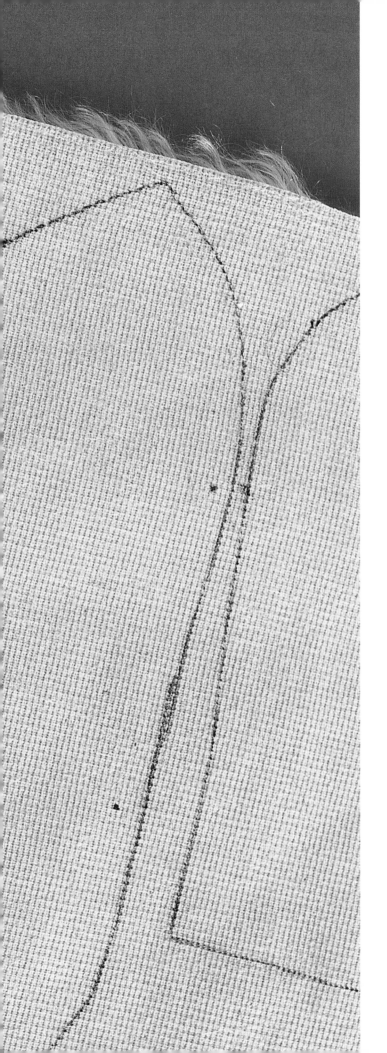

# Patterns

To use the patterns, either trace them with tracing paper and a pencil or photocopy them. As the patterns for Tommy have to be enlarged, a photocopier is ideal. Cut out along the outlines then glue the patterns on to lightweight card to make templates. Mark all important information on the templates, such as openings, and use an awl to mark joint positions (denoted by large black dots on the patterns), as these will need to be transferred to the back of the fabric later. Make templates for *all* pieces, including those that need to be reversed. Transfer each template shape to the back of your fabric using a fine- or medium-tipped permanent marker pen. A 6mm (¼in) seam allowance has been included in each pattern.

For your convenience, the pattern pages have been labelled with the bears' names.

# Albert

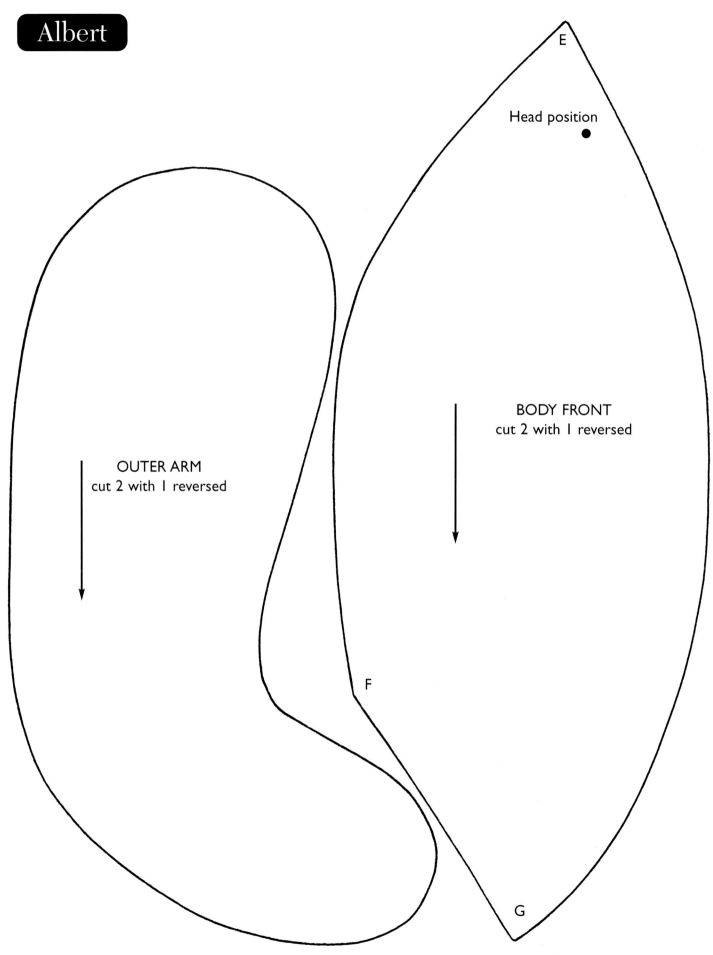

E

Head position ●

OUTER ARM
cut 2 with 1 reversed

BODY FRONT
cut 2 with 1 reversed

F

G

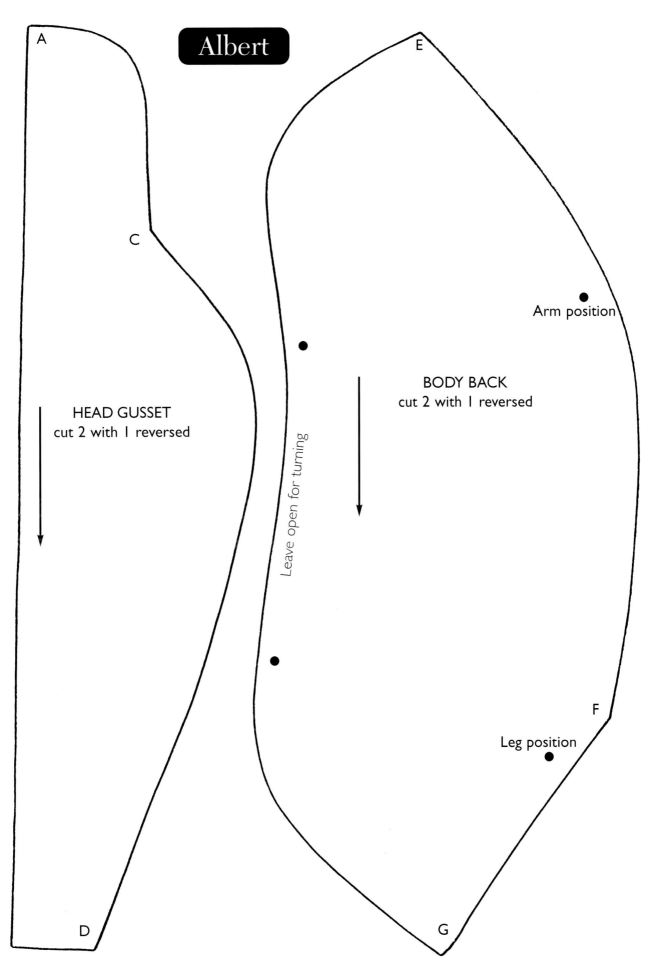

Albert

A

C

HEAD GUSSET
cut 2 with I reversed

D

E

Arm position

BODY BACK
cut 2 with I reversed

Leave open for turning

F

Leg position

G

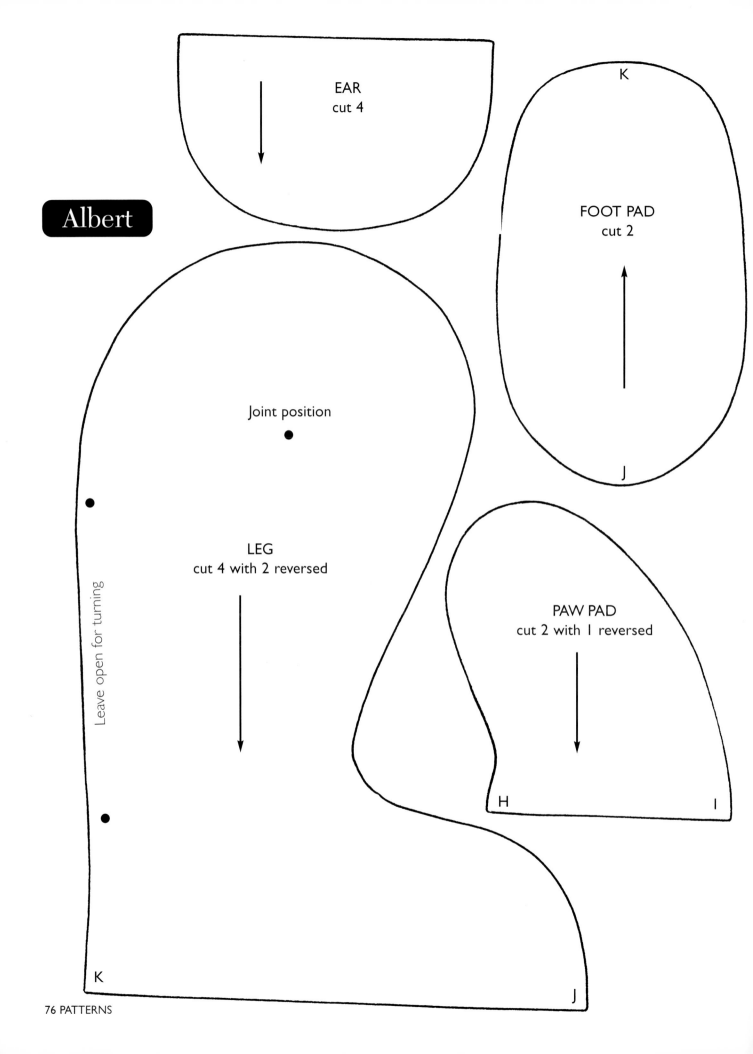

EAR
cut 4

Albert

FOOT PAD
cut 2

K

J

Joint position

LEG
cut 4 with 2 reversed

PAW PAD
cut 2 with 1 reversed

Leave open for turning

H

I

K

J

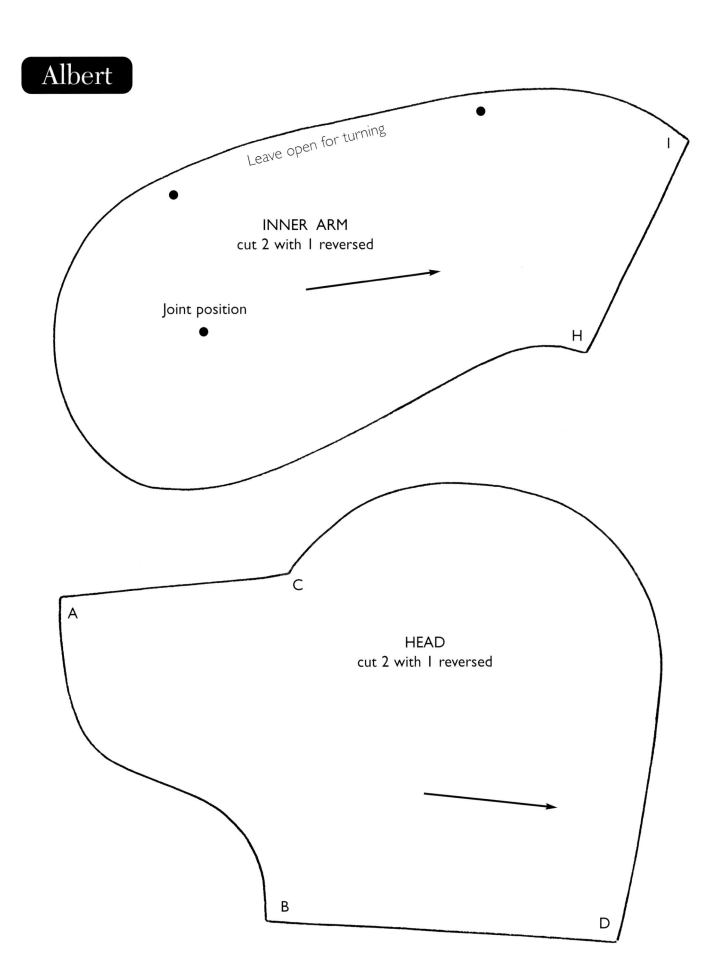

Albert

Leave open for turning

INNER ARM
cut 2 with 1 reversed

Joint position

I

H

C

A

HEAD
cut 2 with 1 reversed

B

D

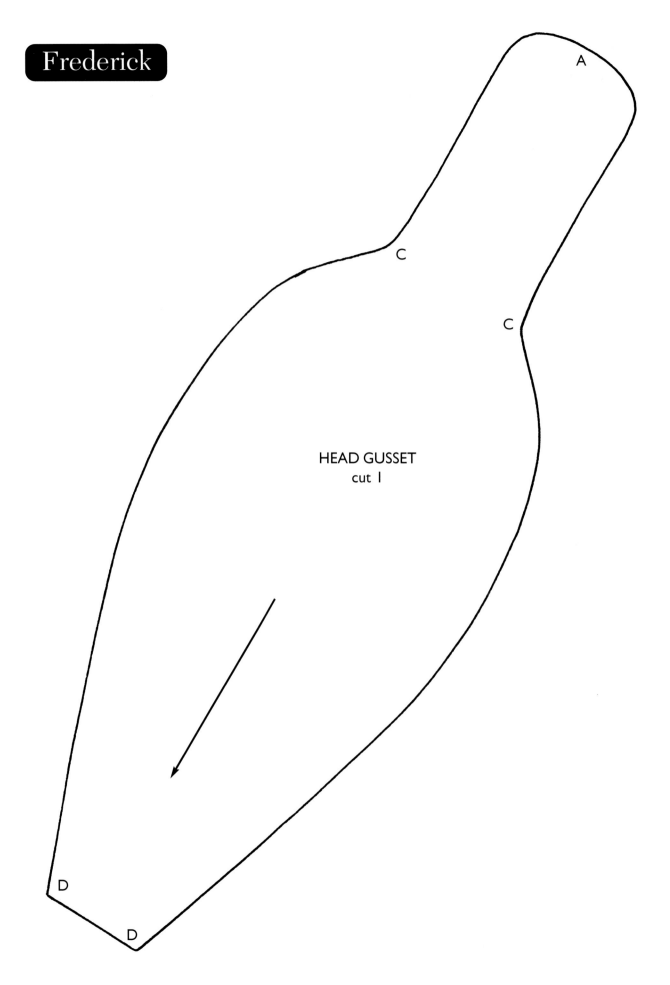

**Frederick**

HEAD GUSSET
cut 1

A

C

C

D

D

# Frederick

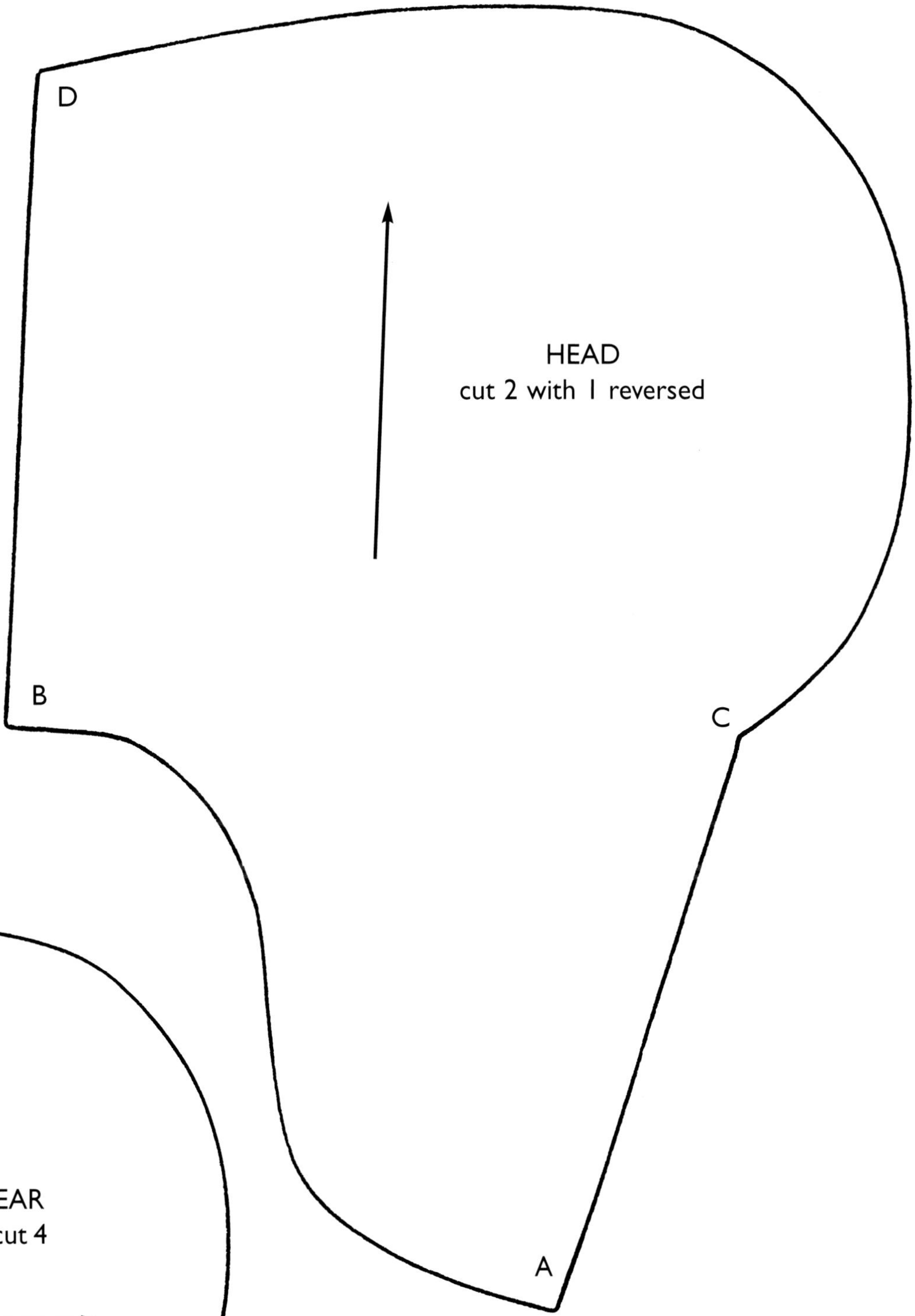

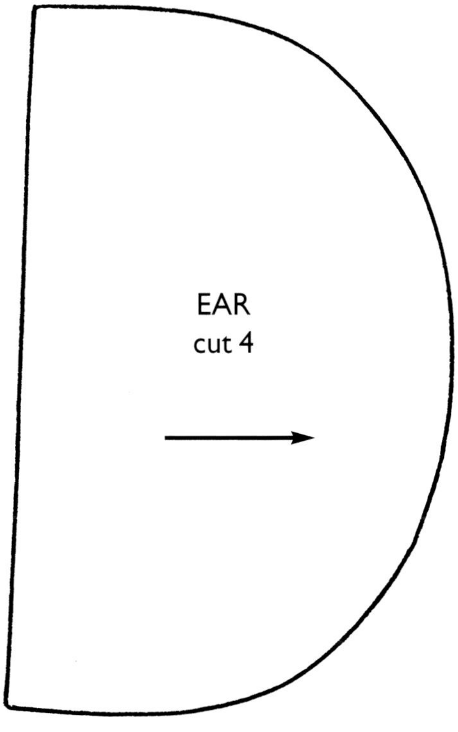

HEAD
cut 2 with 1 reversed

D

B

C

A

EAR
cut 4

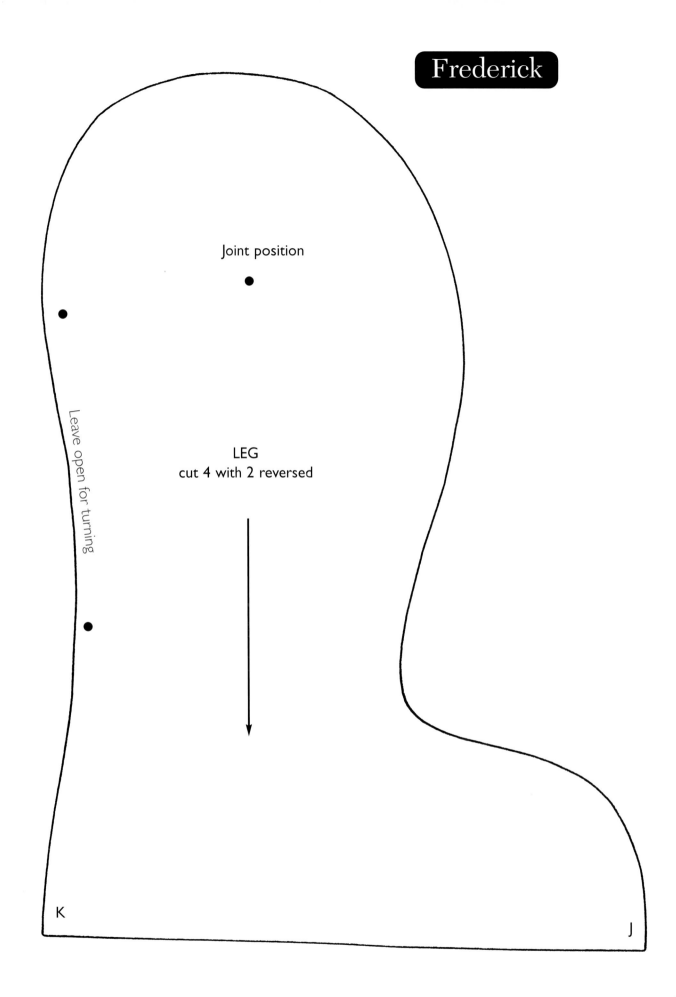

Frederick

Joint position

Leave open for turning

LEG
cut 4 with 2 reversed

K

J

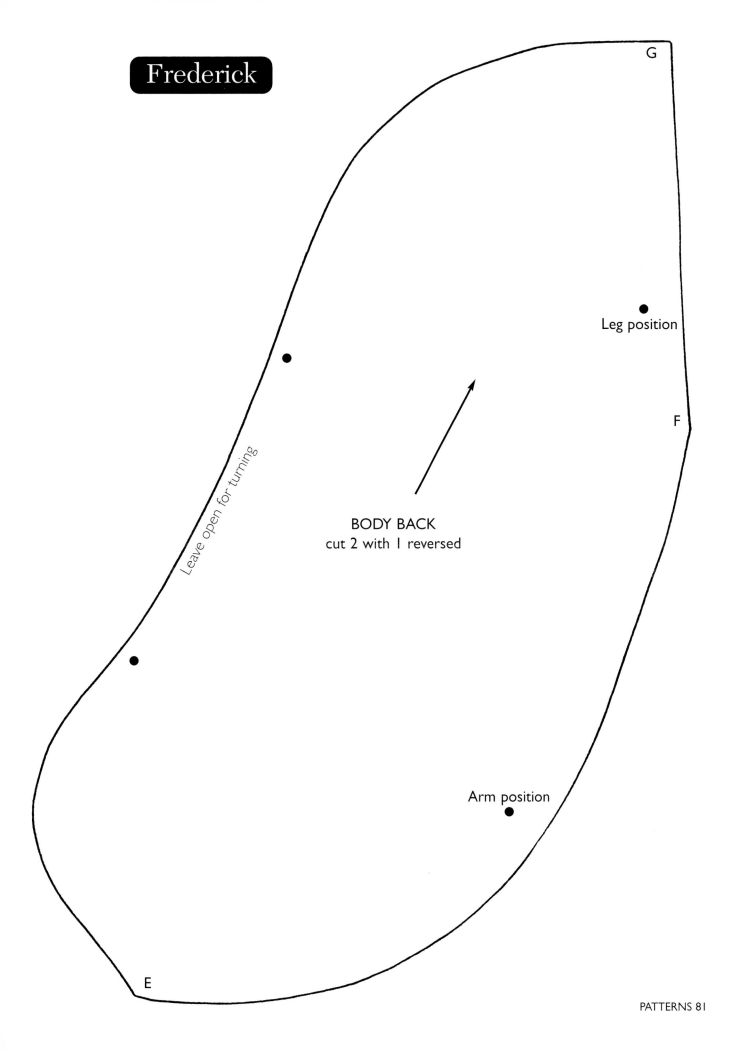

Frederick

G

Leg position

F

Leave open for turning

BODY BACK
cut 2 with 1 reversed

Arm position

E

# Frederick

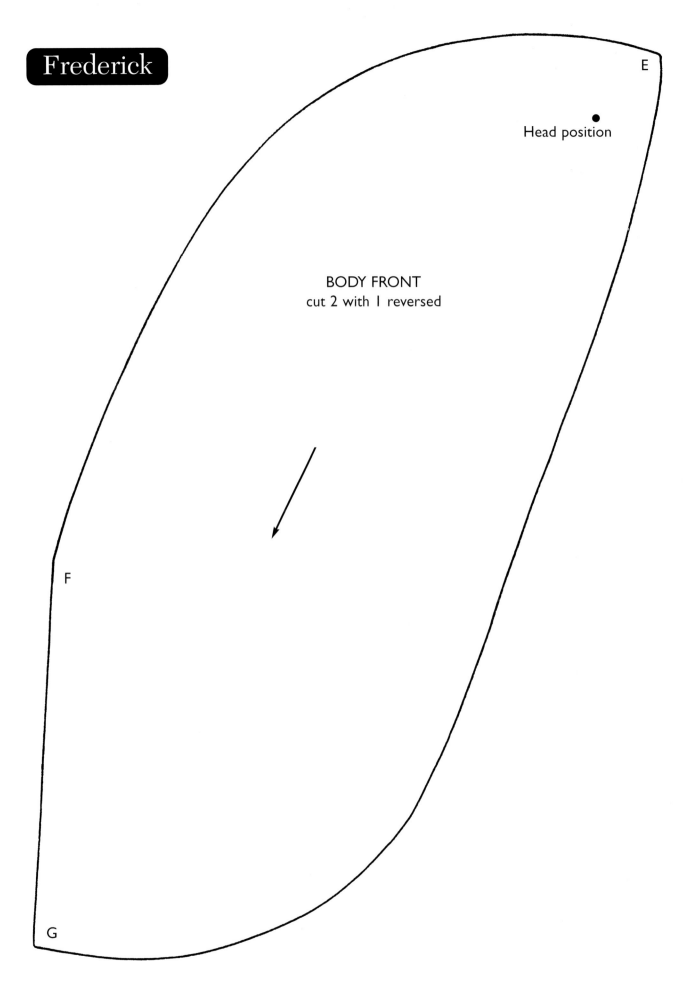

E

Head position

BODY FRONT
cut 2 with I reversed

F

G

# Frederick

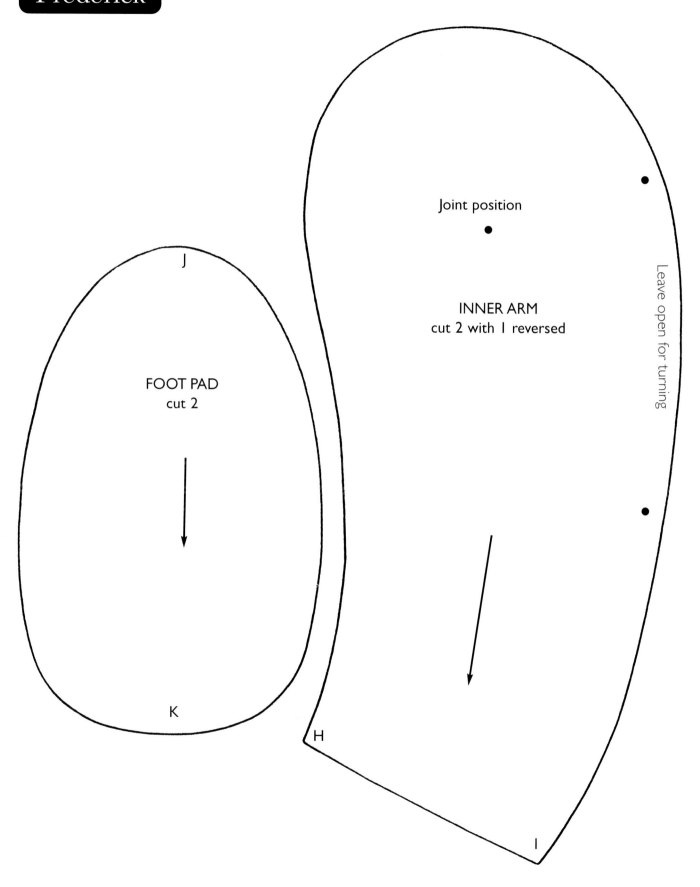

FOOT PAD
cut 2

J

K

Joint position

INNER ARM
cut 2 with 1 reversed

Leave open for turning

H

I

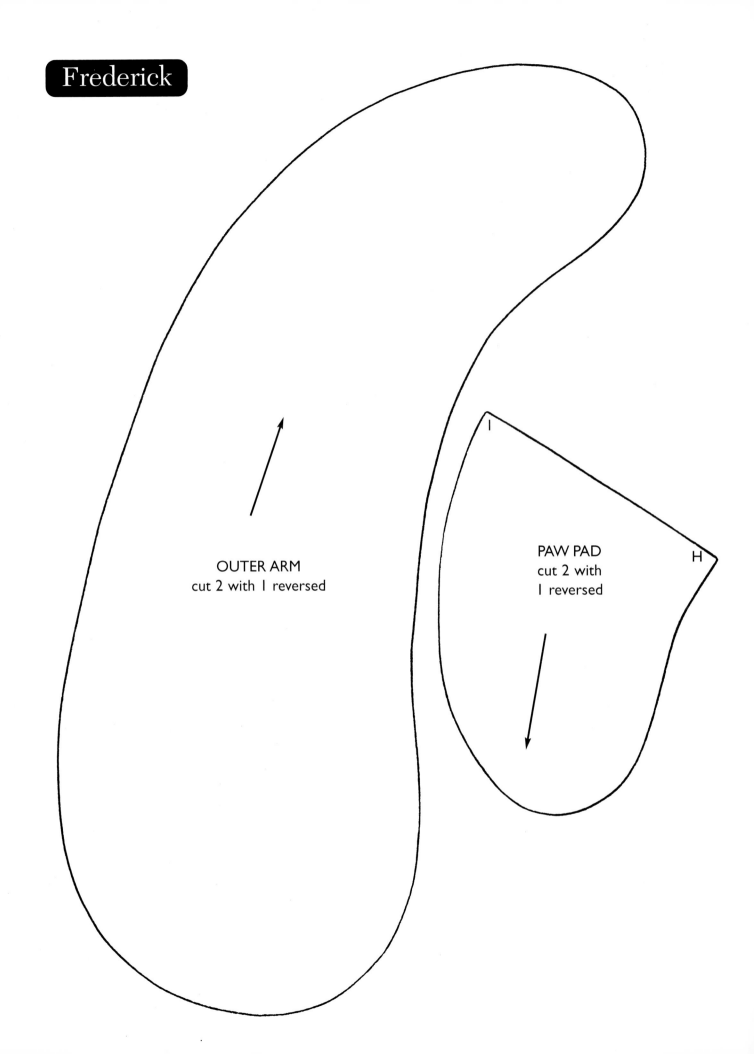

Frederick

OUTER ARM
cut 2 with 1 reversed

PAW PAD
cut 2 with
1 reversed

I

H

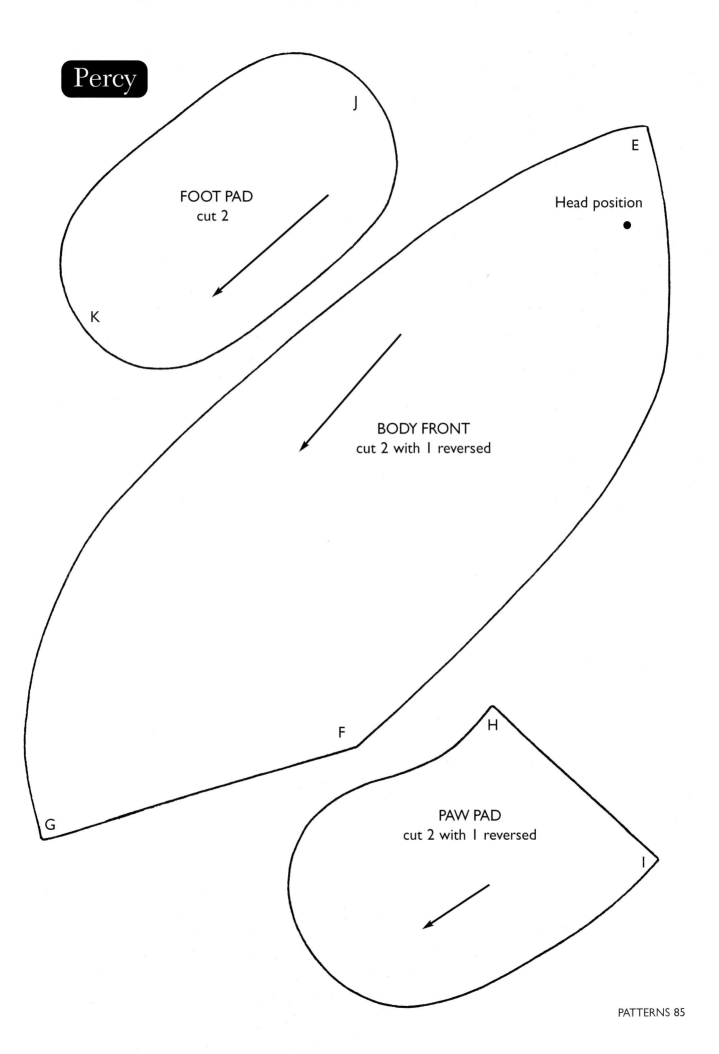

Percy

FOOT PAD
cut 2

J

K

E

Head position

●

BODY FRONT
cut 2 with 1 reversed

F

H

G

PAW PAD
cut 2 with 1 reversed

I

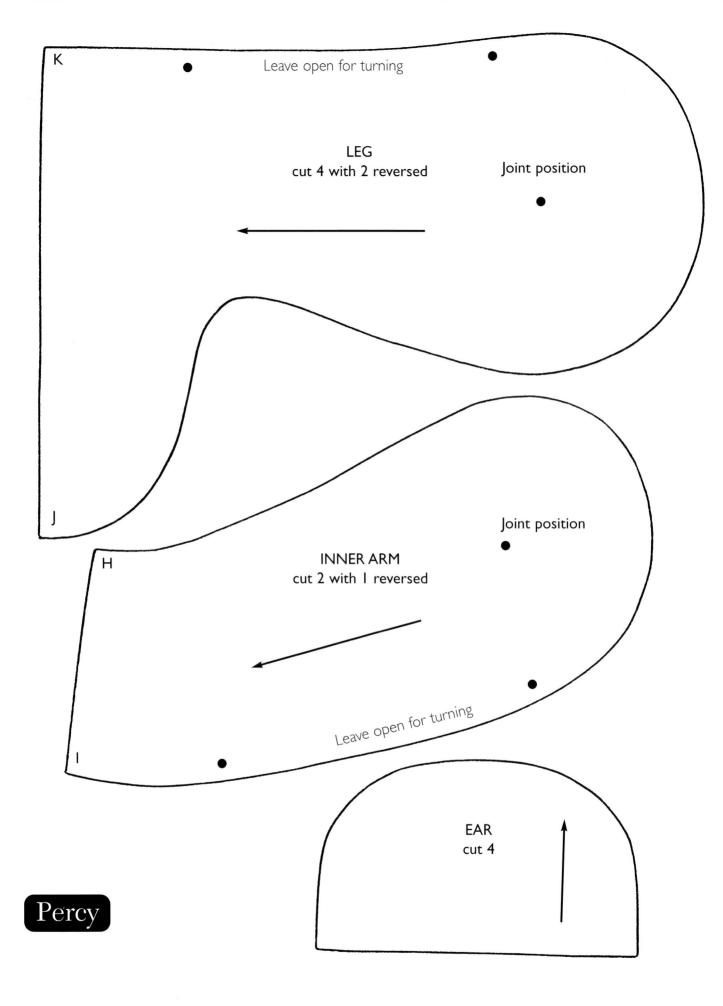

K

Leave open for turning

**LEG**
cut 4 with 2 reversed

Joint position

J

H

Joint position

**INNER ARM**
cut 2 with 1 reversed

Leave open for turning

I

**EAR**
cut 4

Percy

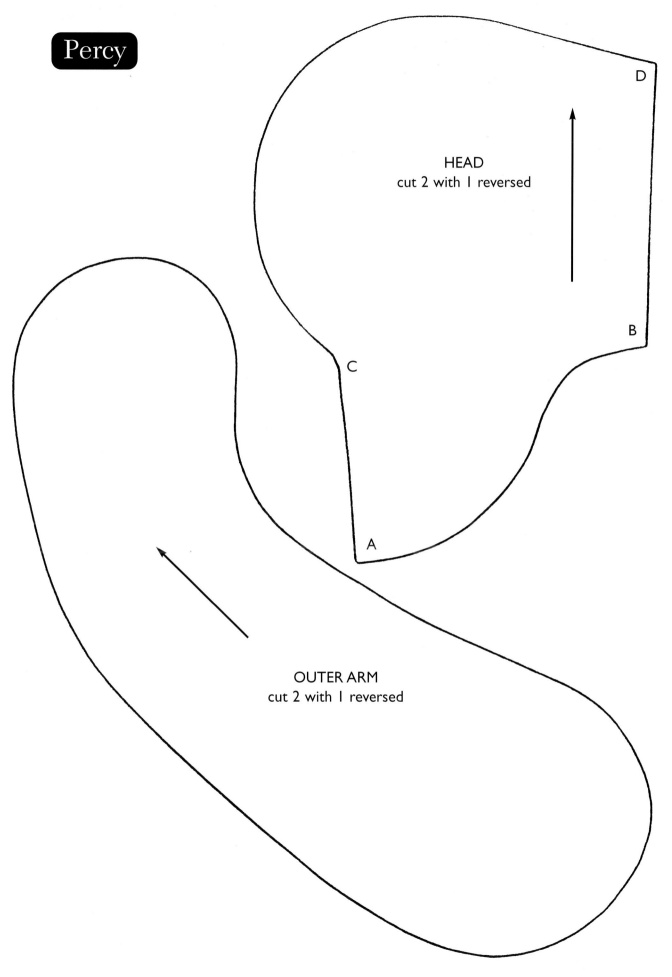

Percy

HEAD
cut 2 with 1 reversed

D

C

B

A

OUTER ARM
cut 2 with 1 reversed

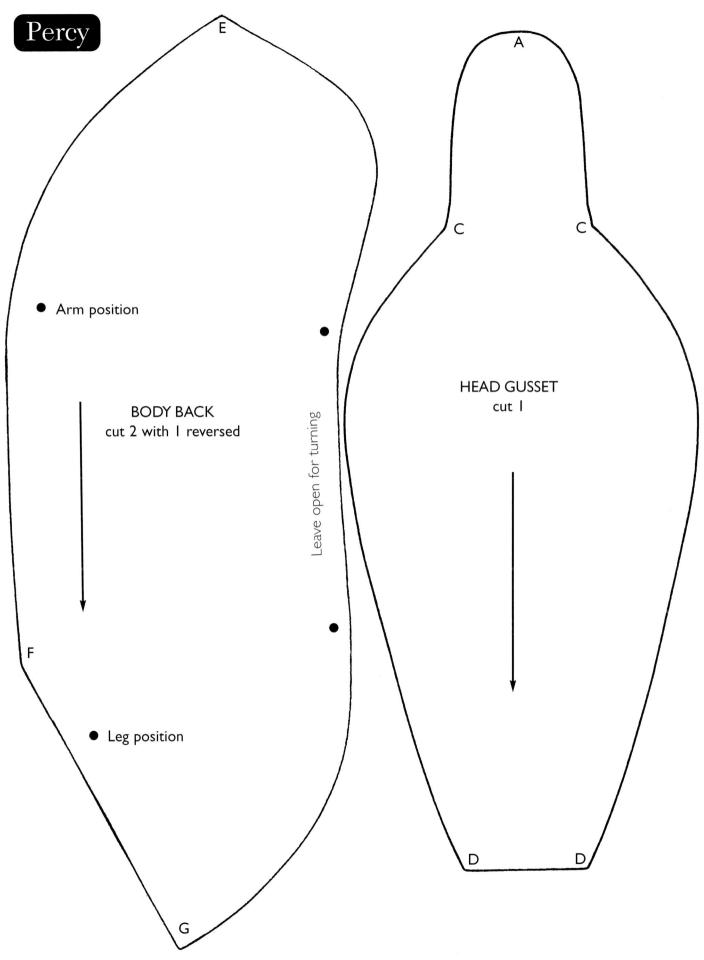

Percy

E

● Arm position

BODY BACK
cut 2 with 1 reversed

Leave open for turning

F

● Leg position

G

A

C        C

HEAD GUSSET
cut 1

D        D

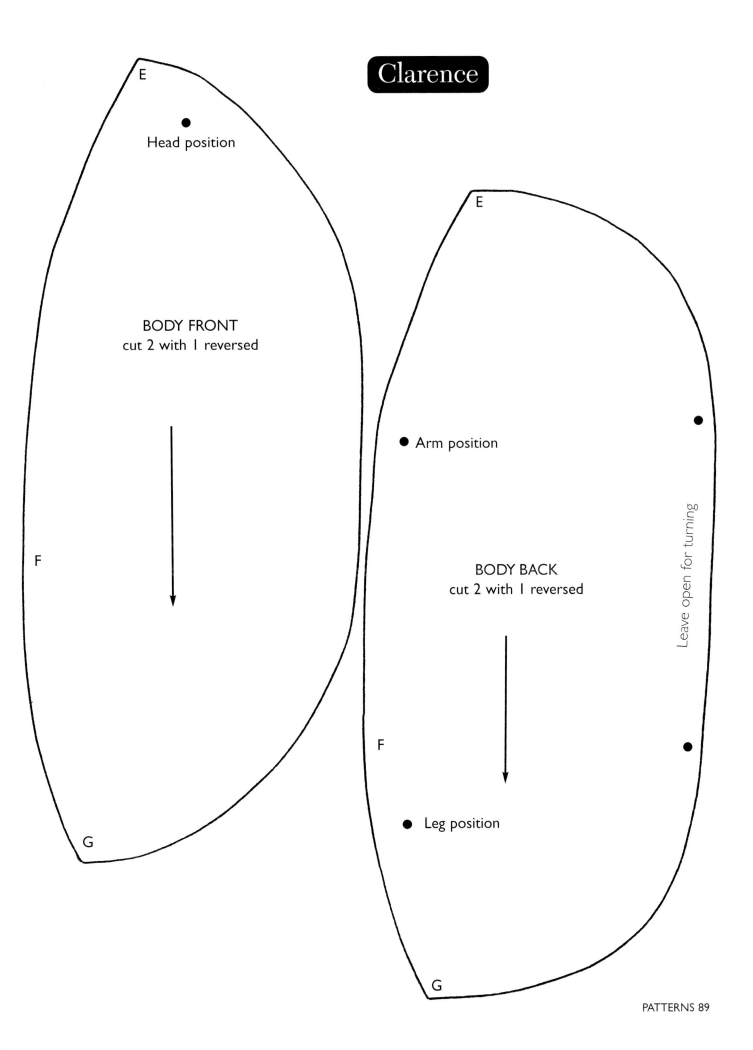

Clarence

E

• Head position

**BODY FRONT**
cut 2 with 1 reversed

F

G

E

• Arm position

Leave open for turning

**BODY BACK**
cut 2 with 1 reversed

F

• Leg position

G

# Clarence

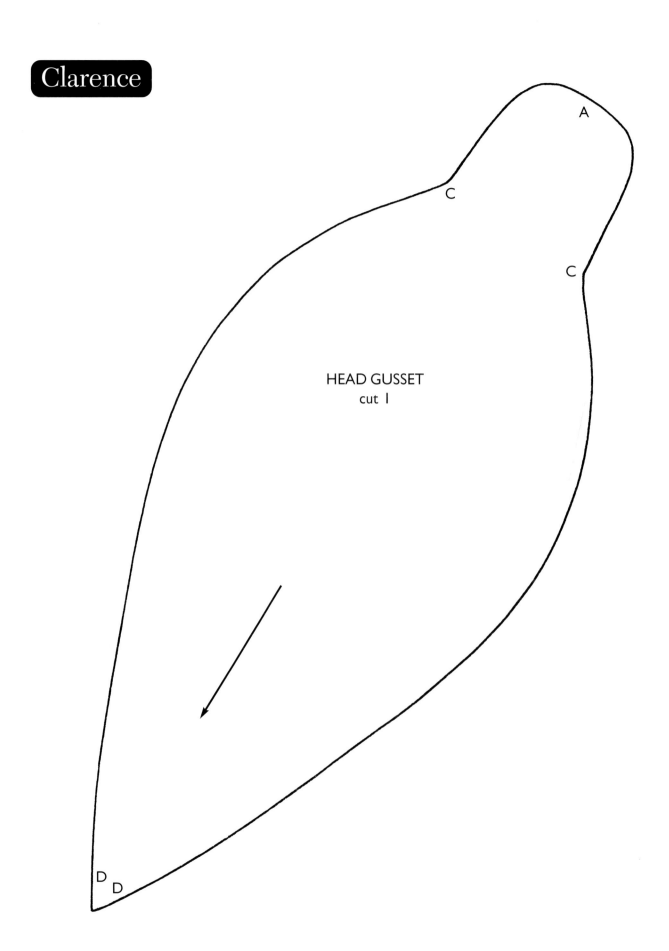

HEAD GUSSET
cut 1

A

C

C

D D

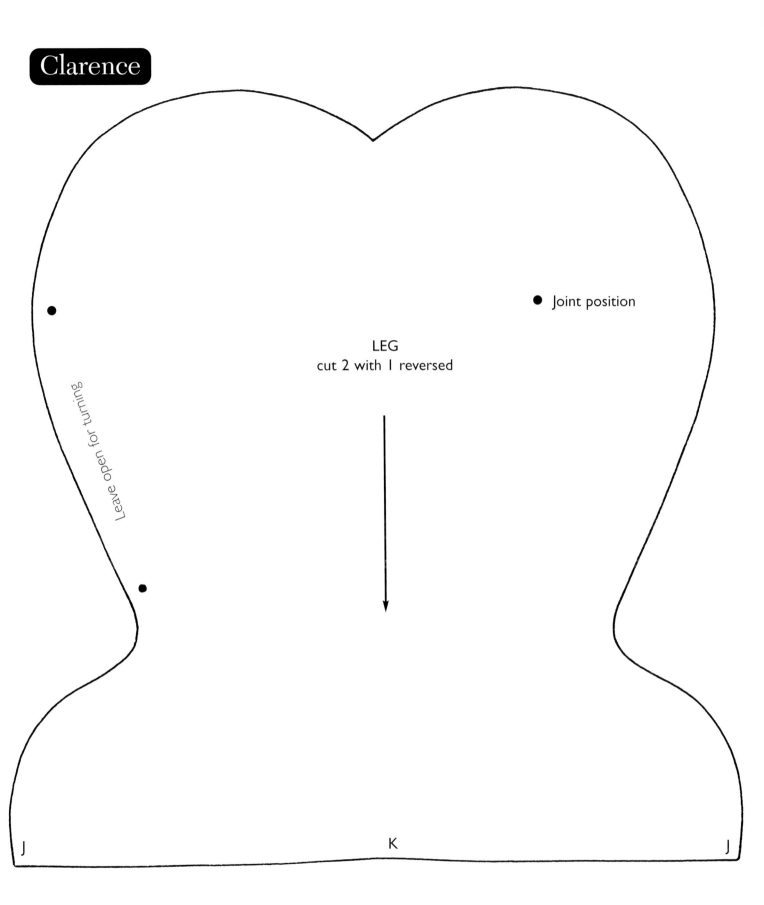

● Joint position

LEG
cut 2 with 1 reversed

Leave open for turning

J

K

J

# Clarence

C

A

**HEAD**
cut 2 with 1 reversed

D

B

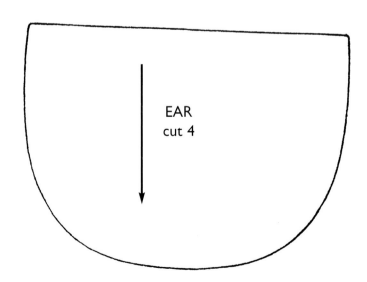

**EAR**
cut 4

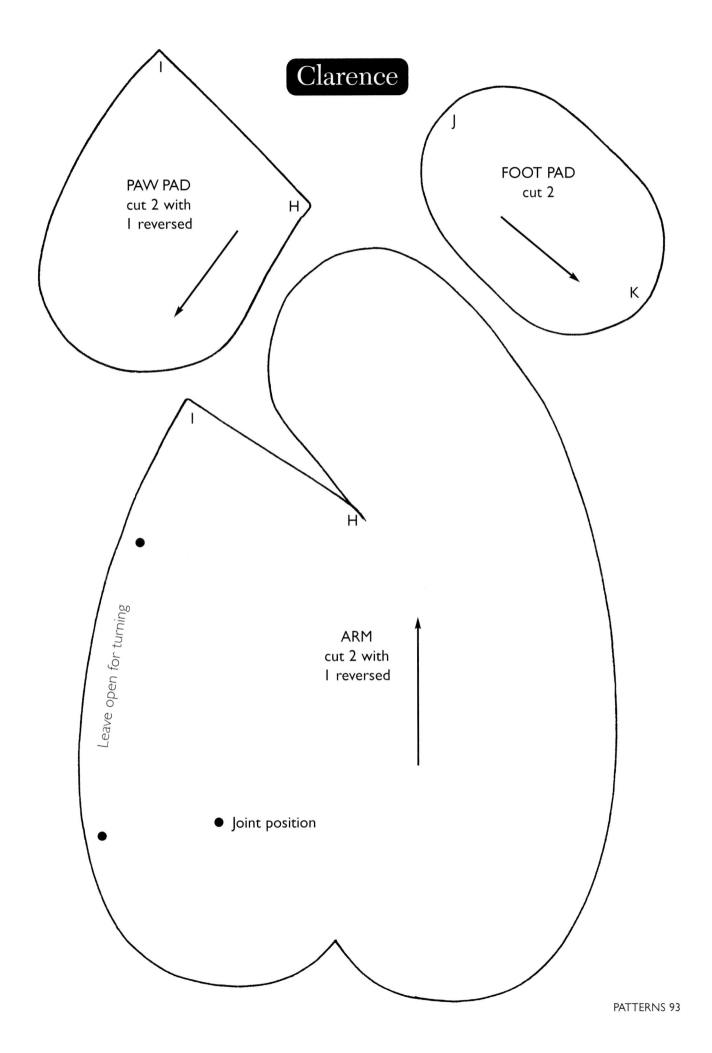

# Clarence

PAW PAD
cut 2 with
1 reversed

I

H

FOOT PAD
cut 2

J

K

I

H

Leave open for turning

ARM
cut 2 with
1 reversed

● Joint position

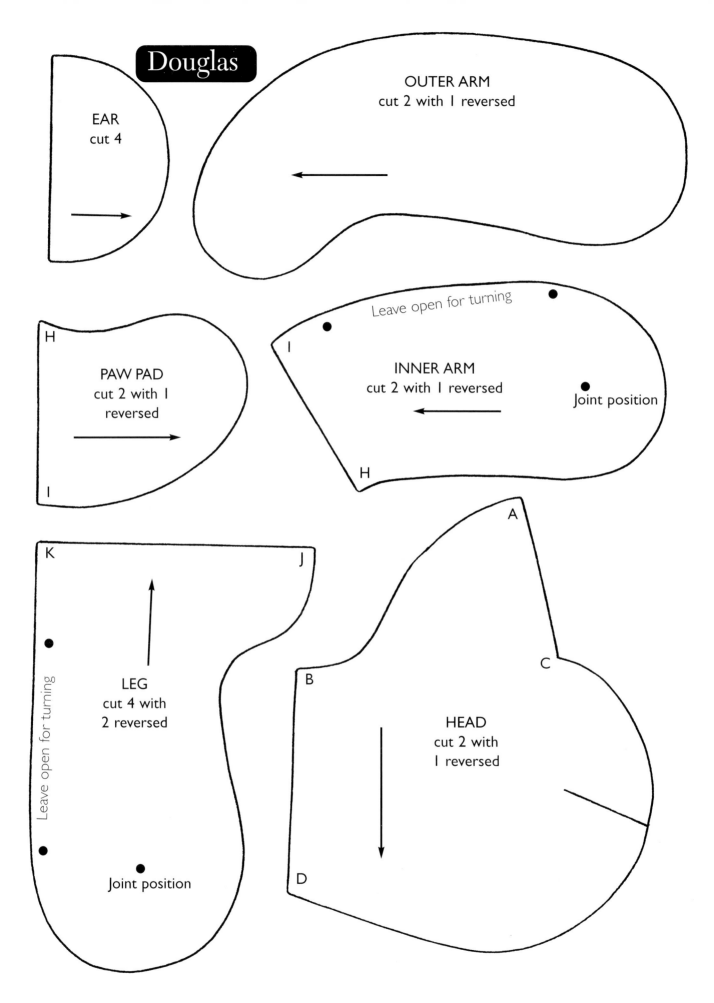

Douglas

EAR
cut 4

OUTER ARM
cut 2 with 1 reversed

PAW PAD
cut 2 with 1
reversed

Leave open for turning

I

H

INNER ARM
cut 2 with 1 reversed

Joint position

K                                    J

LEG
cut 4 with
2 reversed

Leave open for turning

Joint position

A

B

C

HEAD
cut 2 with
1 reversed

D

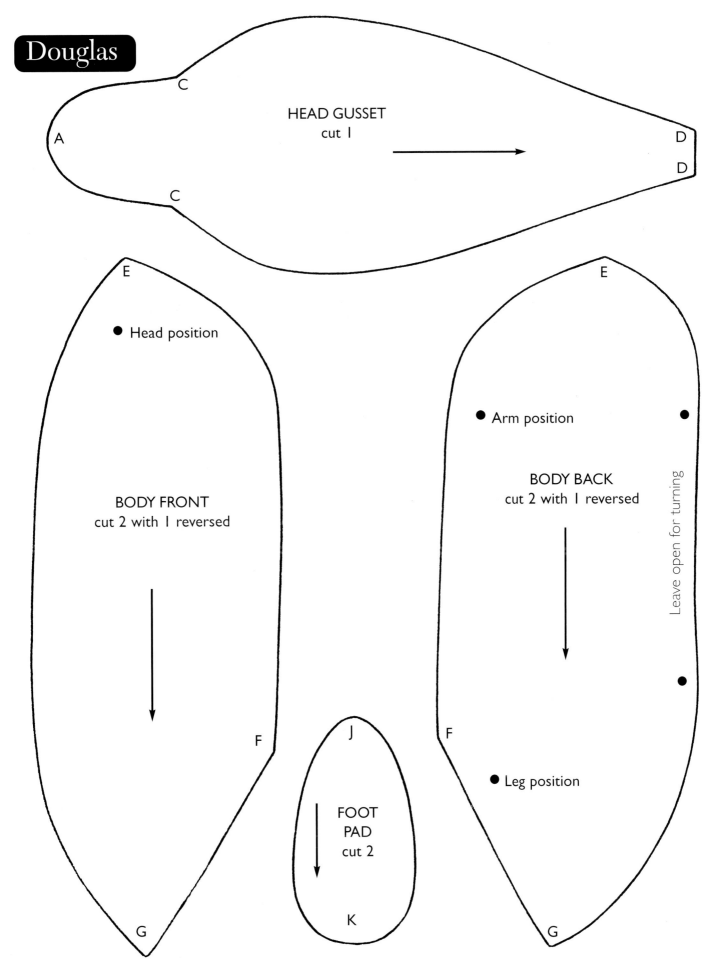

Douglas

HEAD GUSSET
cut 1

A
C
C
D
D

E
E

• Head position

• Arm position

BODY FRONT
cut 2 with 1 reversed

BODY BACK
cut 2 with 1 reversed

Leave open for turning

F
F

J

FOOT
PAD
cut 2

• Leg position

K

G
G

PATTERNS 95

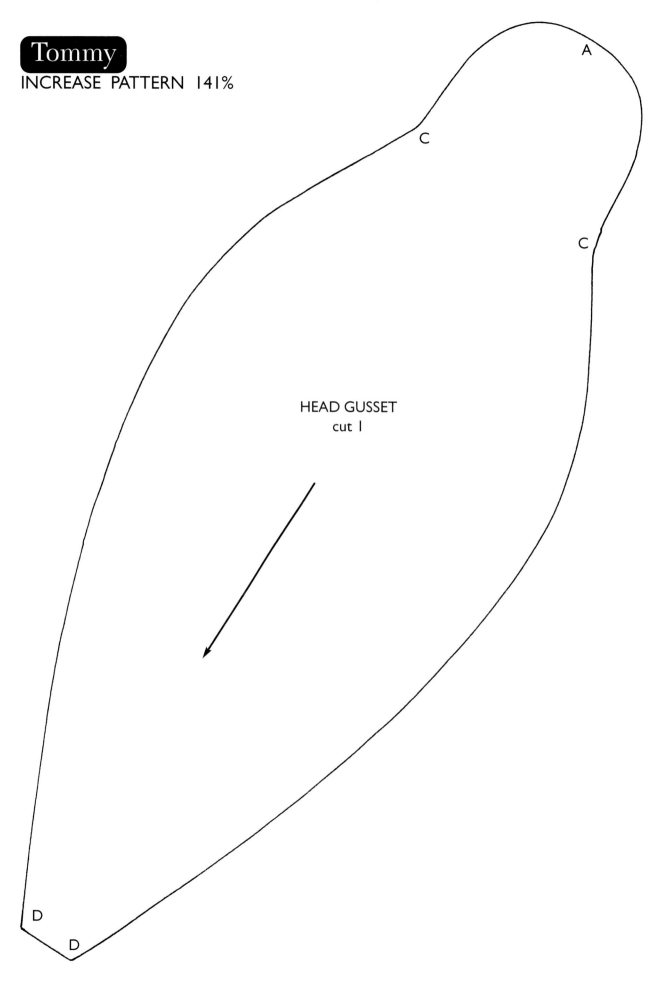

**Tommy**

INCREASE PATTERN 141%

A

C

C

HEAD GUSSET
cut 1

D

D

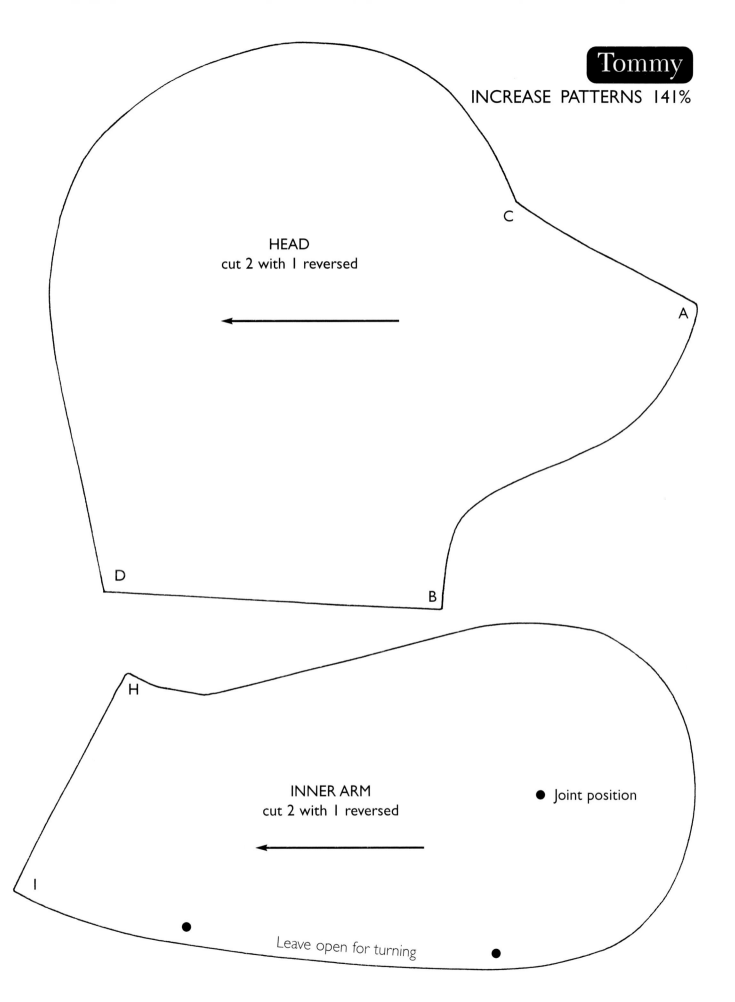

INCREASE PATTERNS 141%

HEAD
cut 2 with 1 reversed

C

A

D

B

H

INNER ARM
cut 2 with 1 reversed

● Joint position

I

Leave open for turning

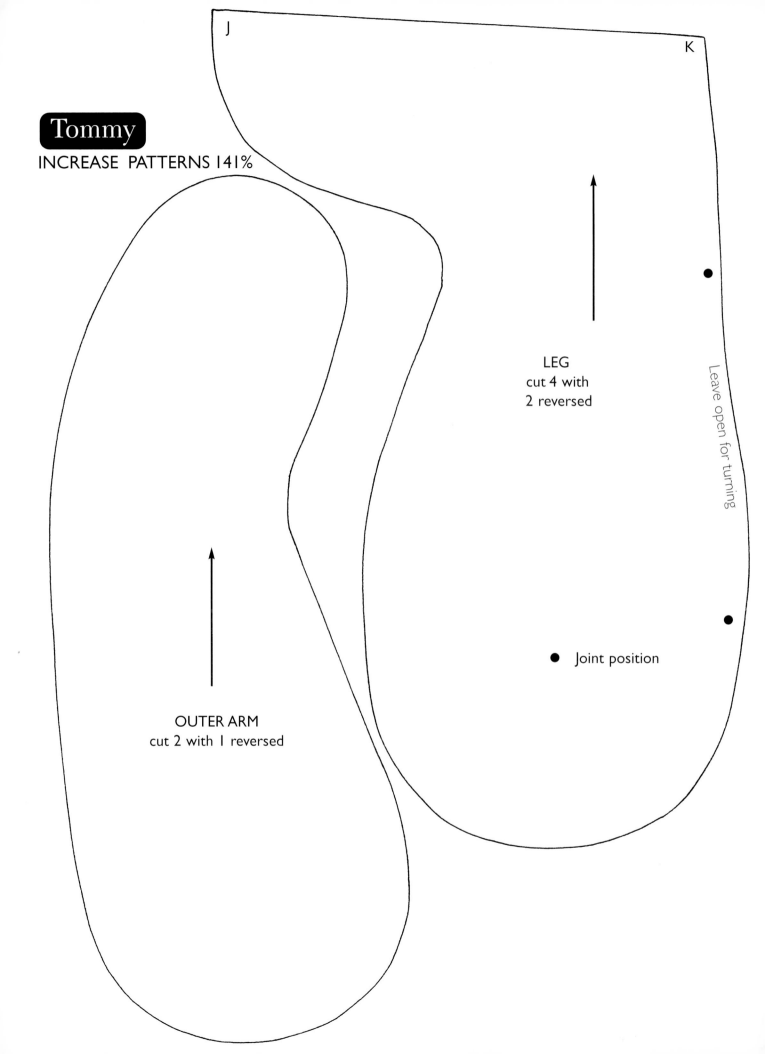

J

K

Tommy

INCREASE PATTERNS 141%

LEG
cut 4 with
2 reversed

Leave open for turning

● Joint position

OUTER ARM
cut 2 with 1 reversed

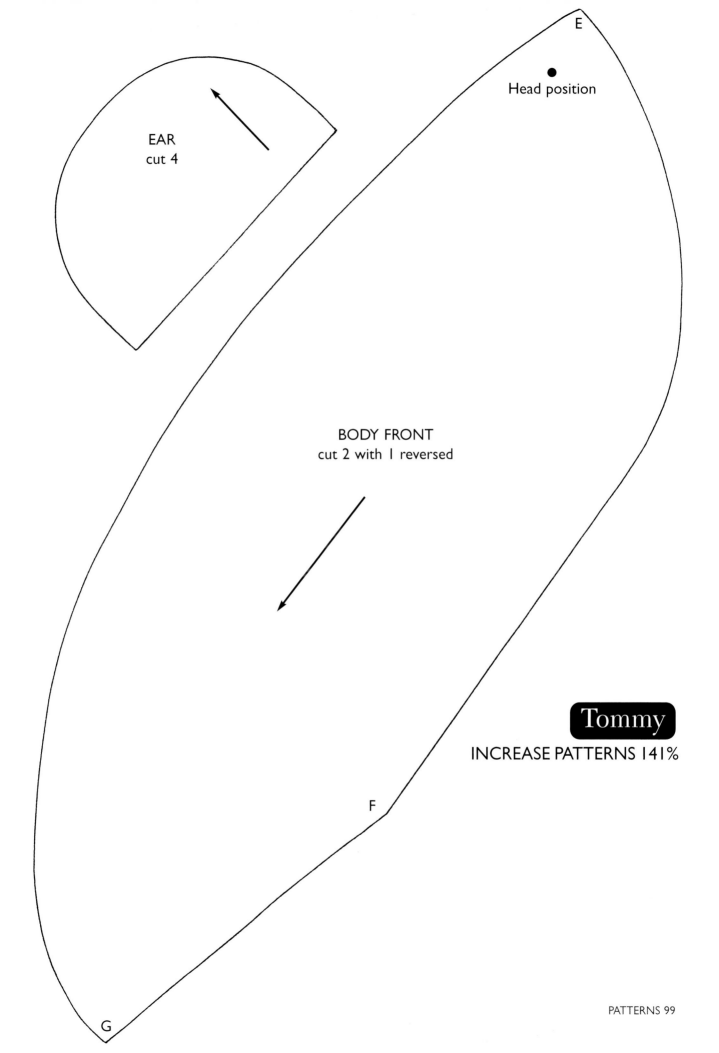

EAR
cut 4

E

Head position

BODY FRONT
cut 2 with 1 reversed

Tommy

INCREASE PATTERNS 141%

F

G

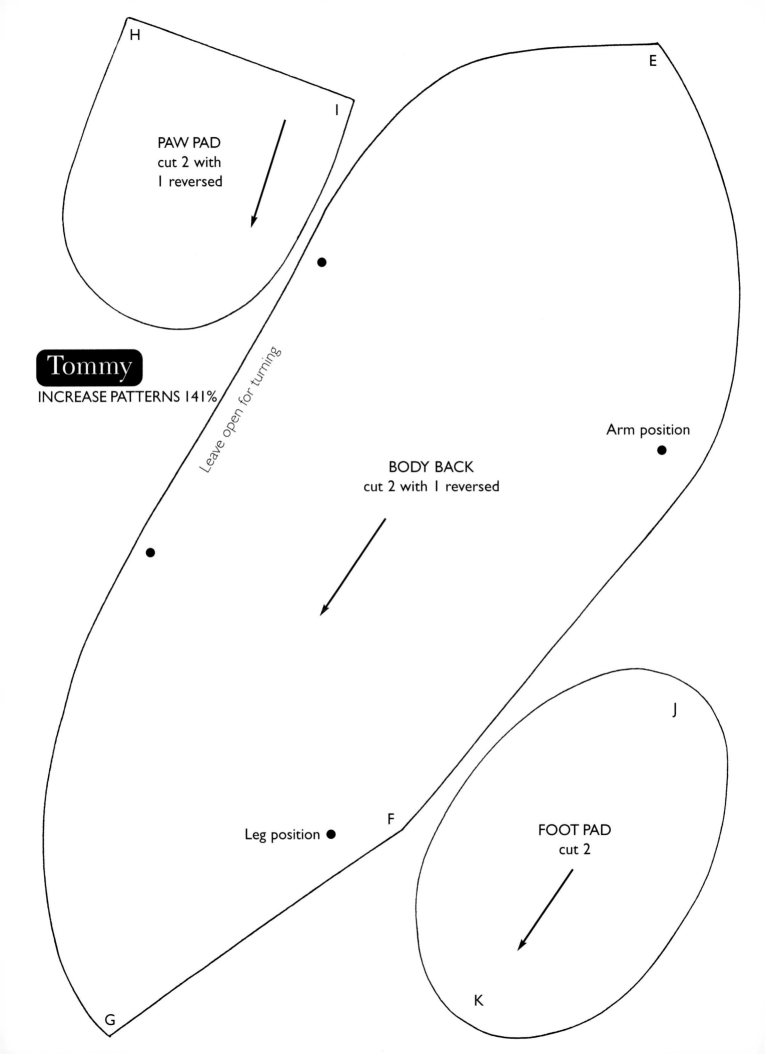

H

I

**PAW PAD**
cut 2 with
1 reversed

K

E

**Tommy**

INCREASE PATTERNS 141%

Leave open for turning

Arm position ●

**BODY BACK**
cut 2 with 1 reversed

●

●

J

F

Leg position ●

**FOOT PAD**
cut 2

G

K

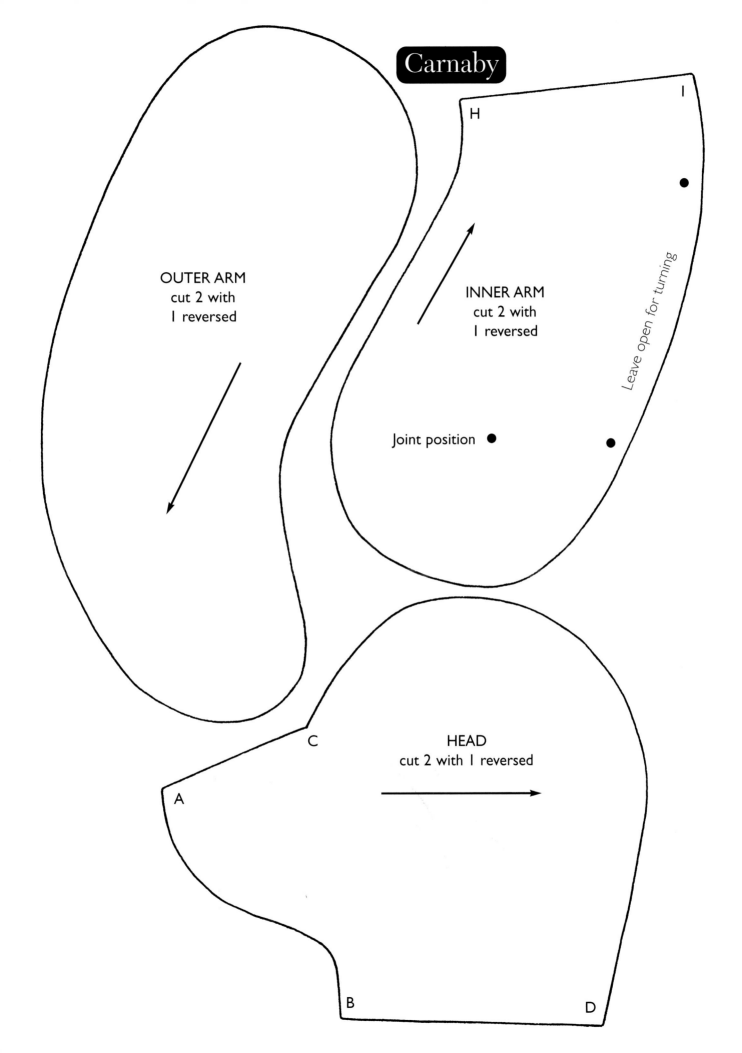

Carnaby

OUTER ARM
cut 2 with
1 reversed

INNER ARM
cut 2 with
1 reversed

Leave open for turning

Joint position ●

H

I

Joint position ●

C

HEAD
cut 2 with 1 reversed

A

B

D

# Carnaby

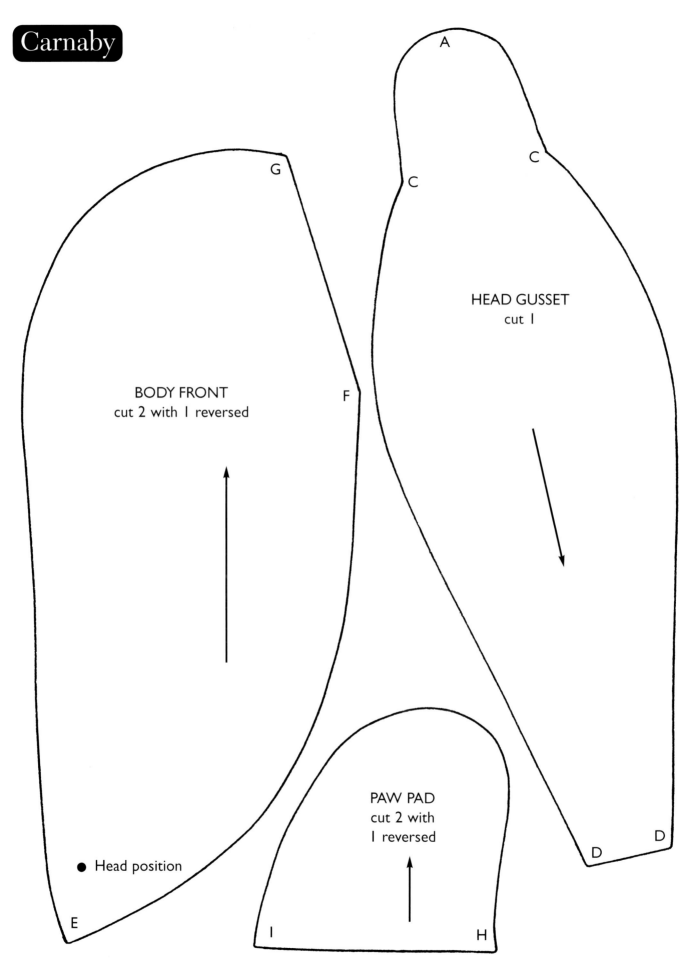

A

C

C

HEAD GUSSET
cut 1

G

BODY FRONT
cut 2 with 1 reversed

F

● Head position

PAW PAD
cut 2 with
1 reversed

D     D

E

I          H

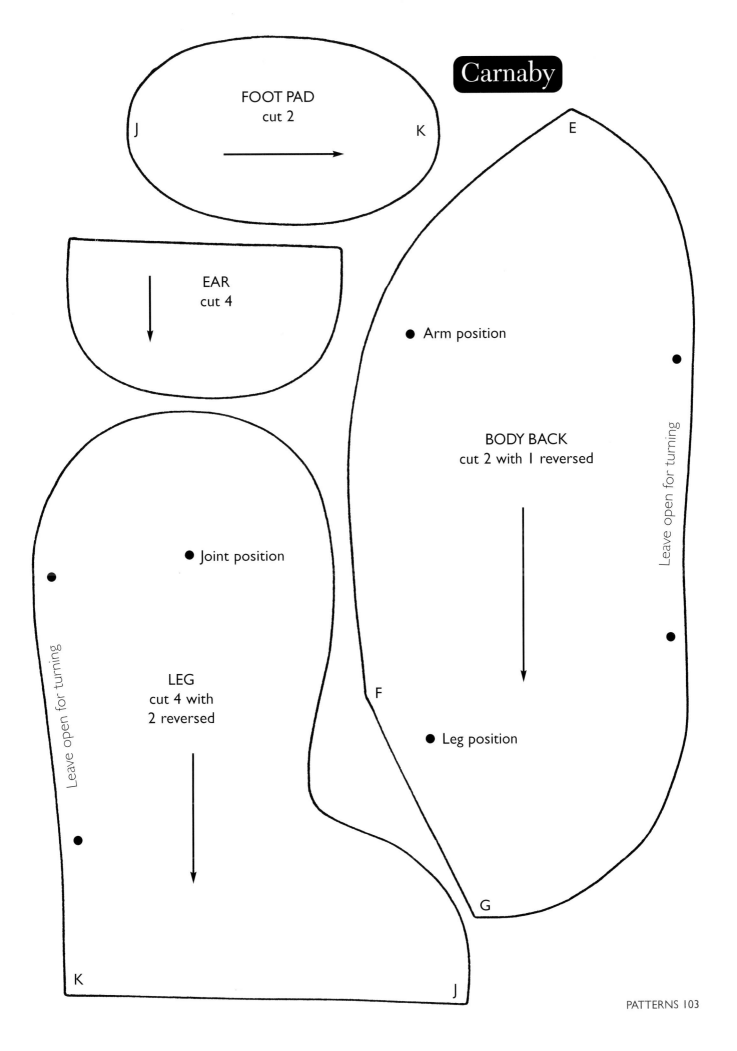

FOOT PAD
cut 2

J                    K

Carnaby

EAR
cut 4

E

● Arm position

BODY BACK
cut 2 with 1 reversed

Leave open for turning

Leave open for turning

● Joint position

●

LEG
cut 4 with
2 reversed

F

● Leg position

●

G

K                                        J

PATTERNS 103

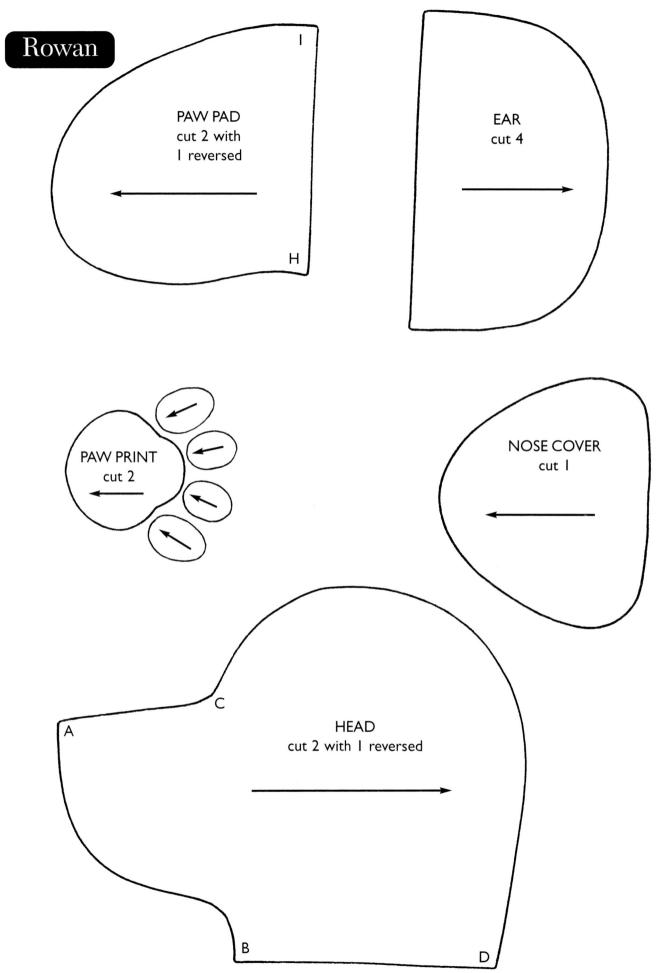

Rowan

PAW PAD
cut 2 with
1 reversed

I

H

EAR
cut 4

D

PAW PRINT
cut 2

NOSE COVER
cut 1

HEAD
cut 2 with 1 reversed

C

A

B

D

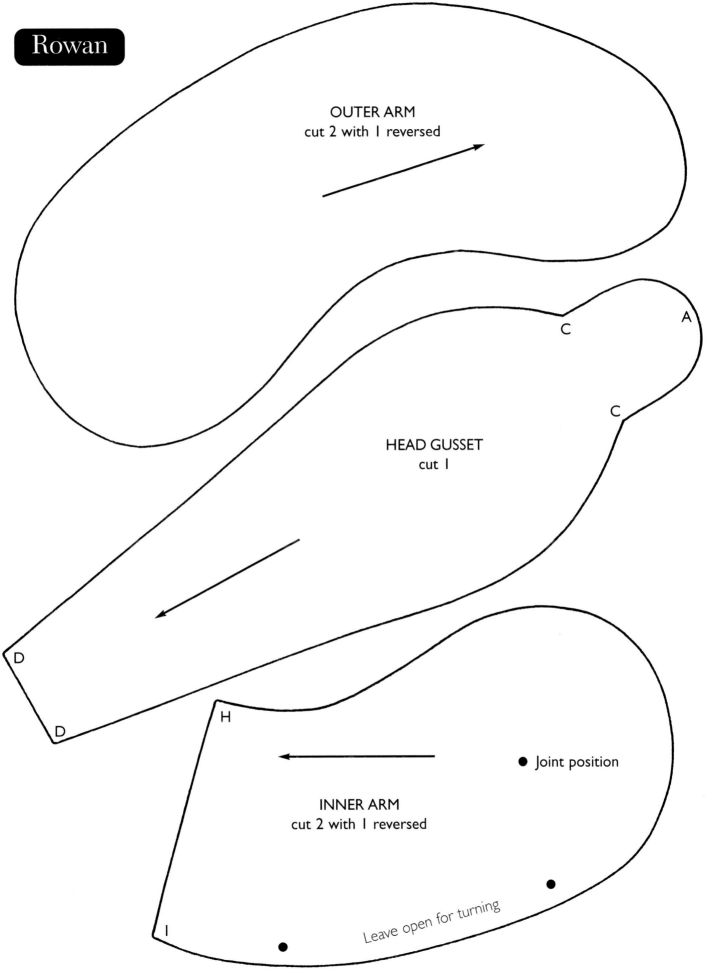

Rowan

OUTER ARM
cut 2 with 1 reversed

C

A

C

HEAD GUSSET
cut 1

D

D

H

● Joint position

INNER ARM
cut 2 with 1 reversed

I

Leave open for turning

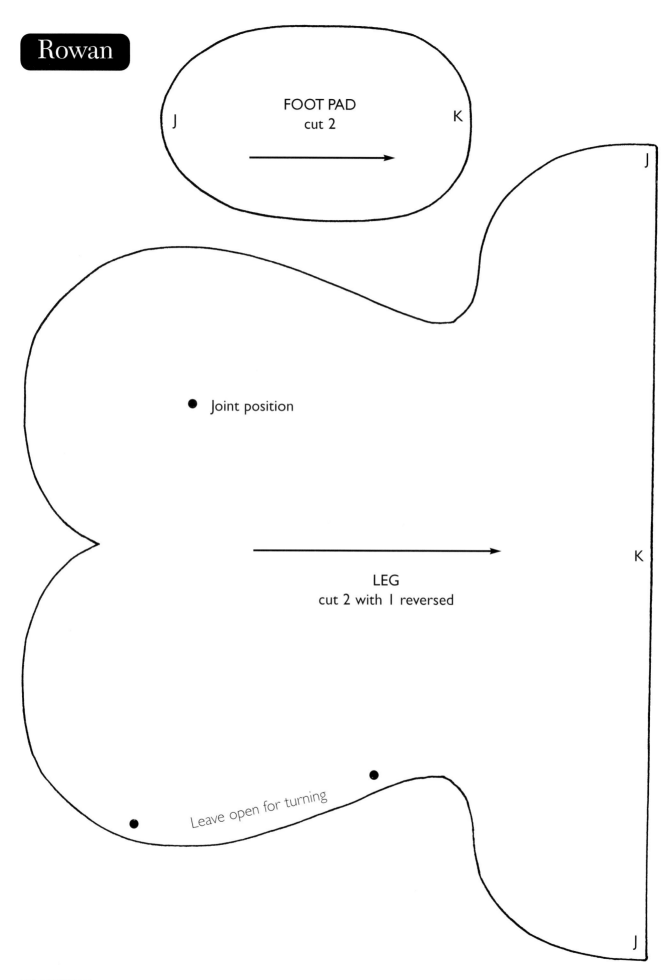

Rowan

FOOT PAD
cut 2

J                    K

● Joint position

LEG
cut 2 with 1 reversed

J

K

Leave open for turning

J

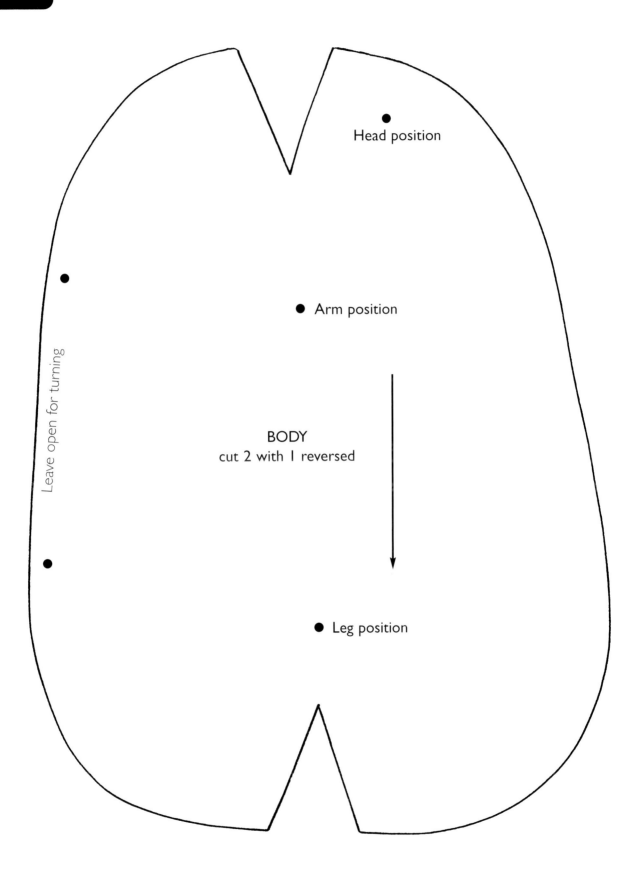

Head position

Arm position

Leave open for turning

BODY
cut 2 with 1 reversed

Leg position

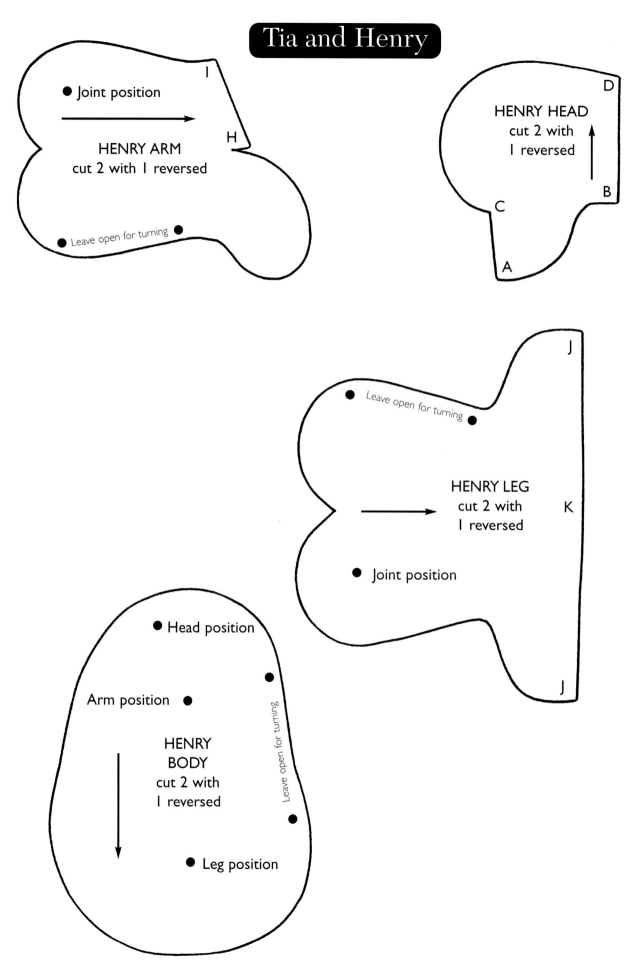

Tia and Henry

● Joint position

HENRY ARM
cut 2 with 1 reversed

● Leave open for turning ●

I

H

HENRY HEAD
cut 2 with
1 reversed

D

B

C

A

J

● Leave open for turning ●

HENRY LEG
cut 2 with
1 reversed

K

● Joint position

J

● Head position

● 

Arm position ●

HENRY
BODY
cut 2 with
1 reversed

Leave open for turning

●

● Leg position

# Tia and Henry

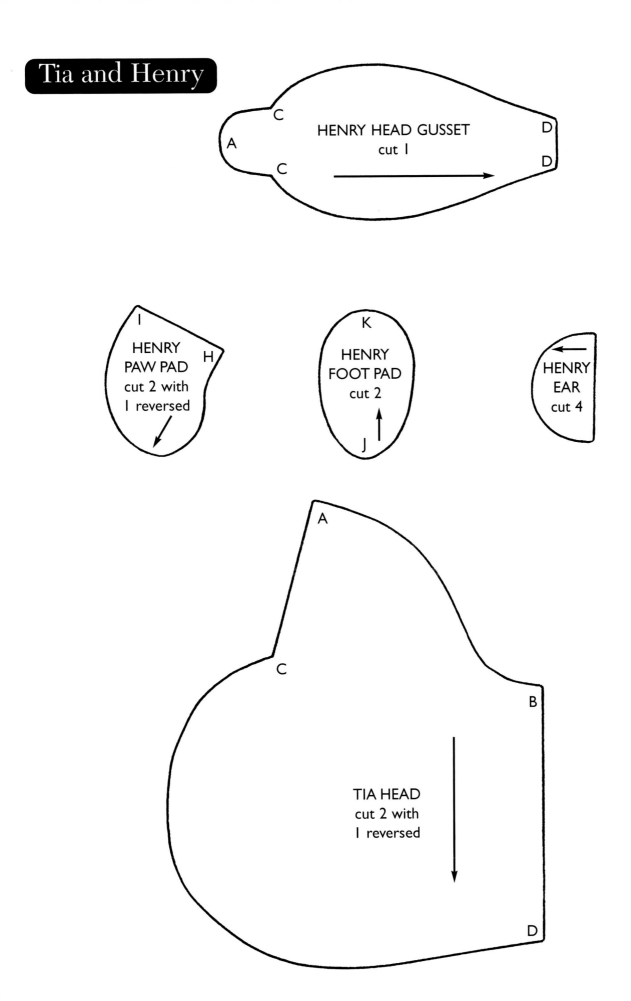

HENRY HEAD GUSSET
cut 1

HENRY
PAW PAD
cut 2 with
1 reversed

HENRY
FOOT PAD
cut 2

HENRY
EAR
cut 4

TIA HEAD
cut 2 with
1 reversed

# Tia and Henry

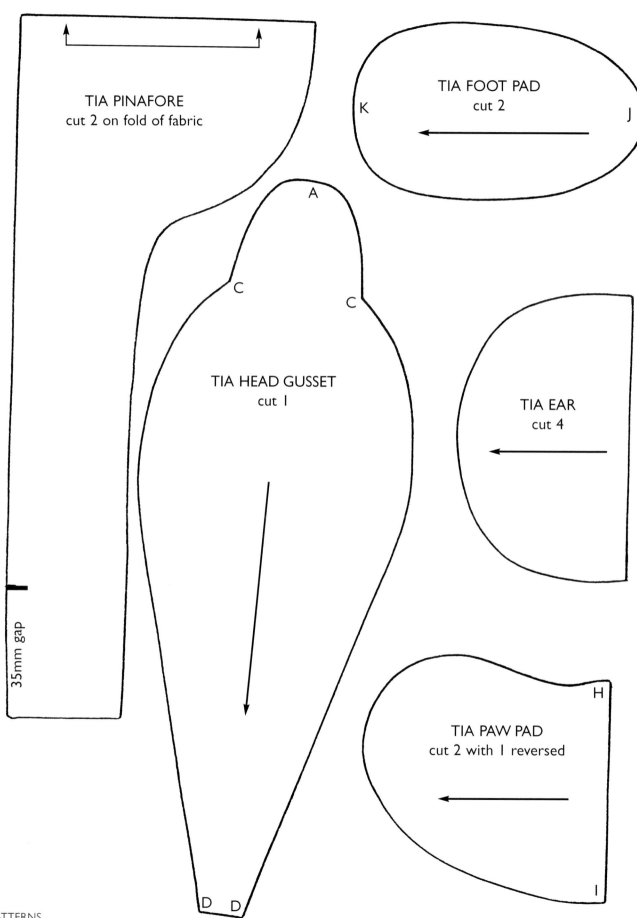

TIA PINAFORE
cut 2 on fold of fabric

TIA FOOT PAD
cut 2

K                    J

TIA HEAD GUSSET
cut 1

A

C        C

TIA EAR
cut 4

35mm gap

D   D

TIA PAW PAD
cut 2 with 1 reversed

H

I

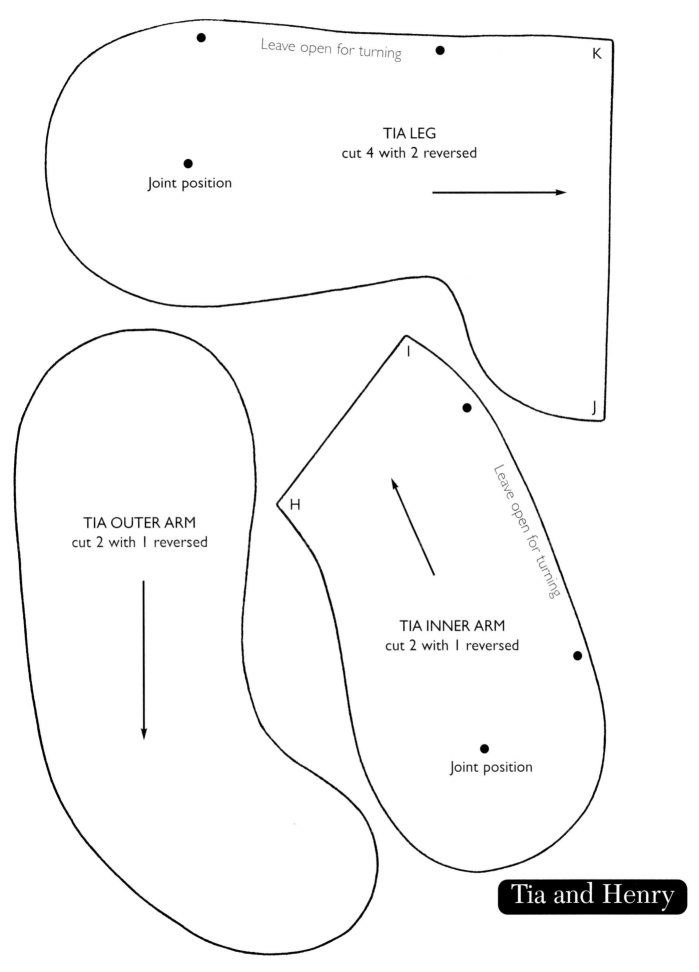

Leave open for turning

K

**TIA LEG**
cut 4 with 2 reversed

Joint position

I

J

H

**TIA OUTER ARM**
cut 2 with 1 reversed

Leave open for turning

**TIA INNER ARM**
cut 2 with 1 reversed

Joint position

**Tia and Henry**

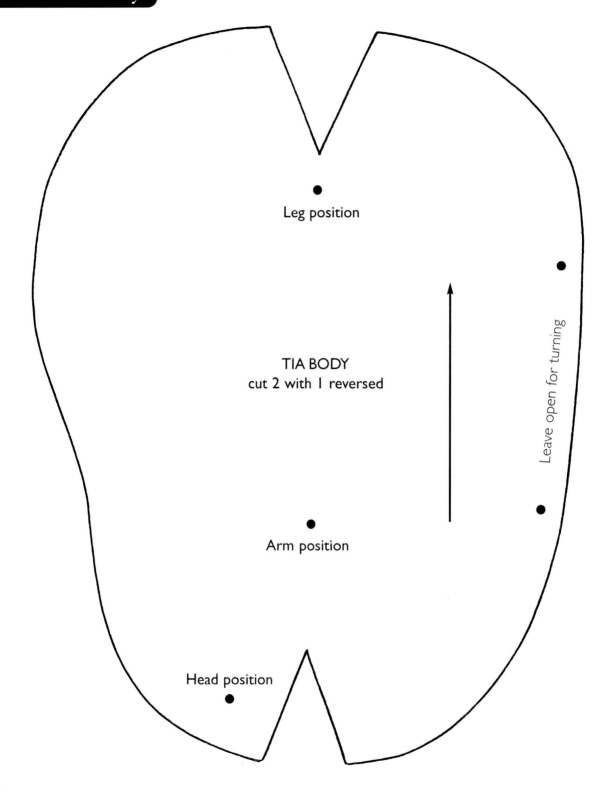

Leg position

TIA BODY
cut 2 with 1 reversed

Leave open for turning

Arm position

Head position

# Honey

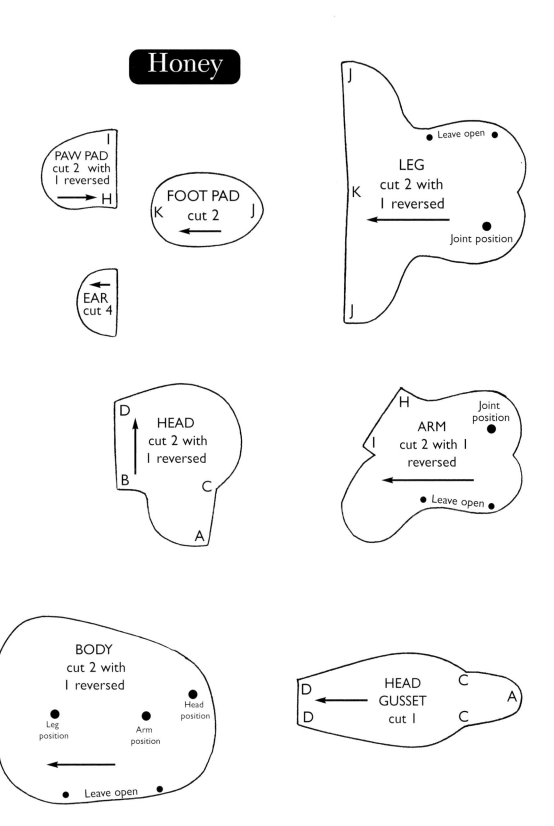

PAW PAD
cut 2 with
1 reversed

I

H

FOOT PAD
cut 2

K

J

LEG
cut 2 with
1 reversed

J

Leave open

K

Joint position

J

EAR
cut 4

D

HEAD
cut 2 with
1 reversed

B

C

A

H

ARM
cut 2 with 1
reversed

I

Joint
position

Leave open

BODY
cut 2 with
1 reversed

Head
position

Leg
position

Arm
position

Leave open

HEAD
GUSSET
cut 1

D

C

A

D

C

# Pumpkin

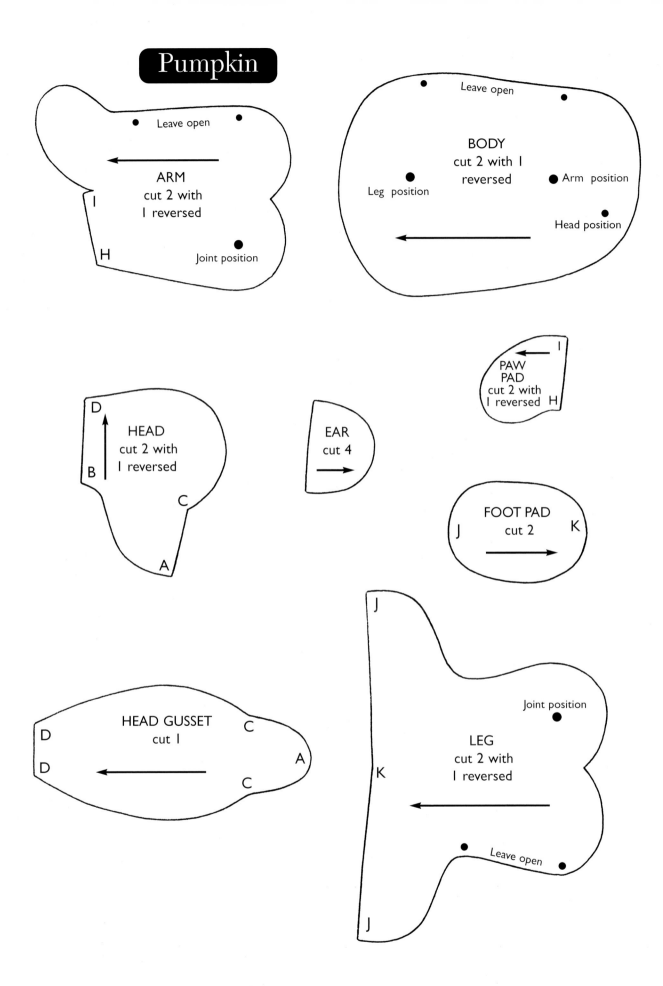

ARM
cut 2 with
1 reversed

Leave open

Joint position

I

H

BODY
cut 2 with 1
reversed

Leave open

Leg position

Arm position

Head position

HEAD
cut 2 with
1 reversed

D

B

C

A

EAR
cut 4

PAW
PAD
cut 2 with
1 reversed

I

H

FOOT PAD
cut 2

J

K

HEAD GUSSET
cut 1

D

D

C

A

C

LEG
cut 2 with
1 reversed

Joint position

Leave open

J

K

J

# Nutmeg

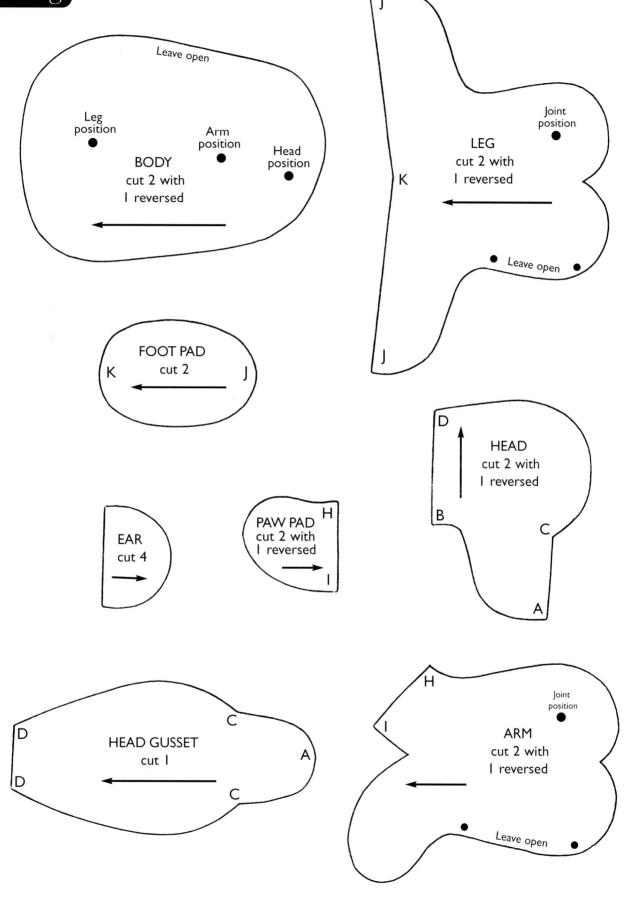

Leave open

Leg
position

Arm
position

Head
position

BODY
cut 2 with
I reversed

LEG
cut 2 with
I reversed

Joint
position

J

K

J

Leave open

FOOT PAD
cut 2

K          J

HEAD
cut 2 with
I reversed

D

B          C

A

EAR
cut 4

PAW PAD
cut 2 with
I reversed

H

I

HEAD GUSSET
cut 1

D

C

A

D          C

ARM
cut 2 with
I reversed

H

I

Joint
position

Leave open

# Manufacturers' History

This is a brief history of some of the more notable teddy bear manufacturers although it is by no means comprehensive. We hope that this insight will give you some idea of the vast interest in the teddy bear.

## Russ Berrie

This enterprise was founded in 1963 in a converted garage in New Jersey, USA. In the beginning, the merchandise was basically novelties along with a selection of figurines but it quickly became established during the 1970s to become a big name in the soft toy industry. By the mid 1980s it became a public limited company and business boomed with their first teddy in 1993, which was traded in Australia under the name of 'Koala Families'. The brother of the founder was Wallace Berrie who started about a year later than Russ but nevertheless went from strength to strength as his business boomed and since 1986 is better known as Applause Inc.

## Big Softies

Fred and Valerie Lyle founded this relatively young British company in 1978 as a family business. Initially they concentrated on the production of realistic life-sized animals and found that 'Big Softies' was a suitable name for the characters they produced. In 1982, however, they introduced the teddy bear after Fred Lyle read a history of the teddy bear written by one of his students as a thesis at college. The name of this teddy bear range was 'Good Companions', another apt name for the product and, as a result, the business grew in popularity and the company soon found itself making bears for department stores as well as for the avid teddy bear enthusiast.

## Gebruder Bing

Two brothers, Adolph and Ignaz Bing, founded this company way back in 1863 in Nuremberg, Germany. At this early stage they mainly manufactured kitchenware and just a few toys but as their ingenuity developed, particularly in the mechanical sphere, the Bing tin toy became extremely popular. Early in the twentieth century, Bing teddy bears started to appear and these caused several legal battles with their rival Steiff, over alleged copyright issues, such as the button in the ear trademark and the mechanical tumbling bears. Sadly, the firm started to decline shortly after World War I and after the death of Ignaz in 1918, his son Stephen took over as company director. Eventually, he left in 1927 after failing to agree with various boardroom members and the company went into receivership in 1932.

## Wendy Boston

In 1941, during the hostilities of World War II, Wendy Boston moved from London to a small place in Wales called Crickhowell. Here, to avoid boredom, she started making an assortment of soft toys out of discarded materials purely as a hobby. This began to prove popular so she developed the ideas and eventually opened a small shop after the war. A year or two later, the expansion of the shop indicated it was now a good time to go into full-scale production and so she opened her first factory in Abergavenny, closely followed by a second in Crickhowell. She went on to market the first machine-washable teddy bear, which was later demonstrated at the Milan Toy Fair in Italy, where the bear was washed in a washing machine and then put through a wringer! Wendy also pioneered the safety eye for toys as well and the company flourished. Eventually Denys Fisher bought out her empire in 1967 and continued production until the mid 1970s.

## Canterbury

Canterbury Bears, truly a family business, was founded during the 1980s by John Blackburn. His wife, daughters and son were all involved in the business whose products quickly grew in popularity, with the firm winning several awards and approvals, including first prize at the First Great Western Teddy Bear Show in San Jose, California, USA in 1983. After this recognition it only took a few short years for production to increase to over 50,000 teddy bears a year! It was in 1987 that the Mayor of Canterbury allowed the prestigious coat of arms of the city of Canterbury, Kent to be used on all the company's labels and paperwork.

## Chad Valley

This company has one of the earliest foundations, being established originally as a bookbinding business in 1820 in Birmingham, England. The name Chad Valley was attributed to the name of a small stream called the Chad that flowed near the factory. Among its many products were the famous cardboard games and soft toys, with the first teddy bear appearing sometime during World War I. In 1920 it was officially known as The Chad Valley Toy Company and went on to acquire numerous other toy manufacturing concerns, including Peacock and Chiltern among many others during the period up to their centenary in 1960. After many restructurings of the company through the 1970s, the Chad Valley trade name was eventually acquired by the massive Woolworth chain in 1988.

## Chiltern

This very famous company dates back to the end of World War I when Leon Rees inherited the old Chiltern toy factory after his father-in-law died. At this time the business was a wholesaler of mainly fancy goods and a few toys until Rees became a distributor of the famous 'Bing' toys in England. Shortly after, a partner, Harry Stone, appeared on the scene and he stayed on as designer and manufacturer of teddy bears whilst Rees concentrated on marketing and sales. In 1923 the first Chiltern bear was marketed as the 'Hugmee' range, many of which still survive today. These soon popularized the Chiltern name and the company succeeded until 1967 when it became a subsidiary of Chad Valley.

## Dakin

This is another small family business which started in San Francisco, USA in 1955, initially as importers of items as varied as shotguns and bicycles! As a result of seeing some packing material in one of the consignments, which was in fact velveteen plush soft toys, it was quickly realized that the market for such toys was at that time very lucrative. The company grew from then on but sadly a tragic air crash killed many members of the Dakin family. By 1970, after reorganization of the company, production was moved to Korea and it flourished again. At the end of the 1980s, Dakin acquired House of Nisbet and by the 1990s exports were being sent to more than eighty countries.

## Deans

This British company was started in 1903 selling rag books for children, which were a great success. In later years the company had a logo designed that depicted two dogs fighting over one of its books. In 1908 its first successful bear was launched. After rapid expansion right through until the mid 1960s it flourished and the company was renamed Deans' Childsplay Toys Ltd. It celebrated its 80th birthday in 1983 but in 1988 went into voluntary liquidation at which point Neil Miller, the then managing director of a year or so, bought the trading rights and began trading as The Deans Company (1903). Then in 1990 he managed to secure the original company, Deans

Rag Book Co Ltd. The replica bears were an instant hit and today the company is one of the most well known teddy bear manufacturers.

## Farnell

J.K. Farnell originally made pincushions and tea-cosies when the company was formed in 1840 in London, England. It produced soft toys at the end of the nineteenth century, with the first teddy bear appearing in 1908. In the 1920s business thrived and in 1925 its 'Alpha' label was officially accepted as a trademark. Expansion soon followed and wheeled toys were developed. Sales reached New York and Paris but in 1934 the factory was destroyed by fire. It was rebuilt a year later only to be destroyed again during wartime. After hostilities ceased, production grew again and by the end of the 1950s, ninety-five per cent of production was for export! A feat indeed. However during the 1960s things changed for Farnell and by 1968 the company had been bought out by a finance company.

## Gund

This company was founded in Connecticut, USA by a German immigrant, Adolph Gund, in 1898. Initially making novelty goods, belts and so on, it soon recognized the appeal of the teddy bear and produced its first bear in 1906. This initial range of four bears was so successful that like many other teddy bear manufacturers of the time, success was virtually guaranteed and business boomed right through the 1920s, when mechanical animals were added to their range of toys. By the late 1940s the company had secured exclusive rights with Walt Disney to produce soft toy versions of the Disney cartoons. After several moves and expansions, it entered the 'Collector's Bear' market in 1979. This secured a firm footing for Gund in the teddy bear market and in 1992 it became distributor for Canterbury Bears both in the USA and Canada.

## Hermann

There are currently two Hermann names in the teddy bear world – Hermann Spielwaren and Gebruder Hermann. Both are related and were founded in Germany but Hermann Spielwaren was the first, being founded in 1913. Both were complete family businesses and specialized in quality teddy bears with limited editions aimed at the collectors' market. After many years of relative hardship due to political pressures, today the Hermann name is recognized world-wide as a manufacturer of the jointed traditional teddy bear.

## Ideal

The Ideal Novelty & Toy Company was the company who many believe founded the teddy bear as we know it today, in 1903 after the famous Berryman cartoon depicting President 'Teddy' Roosevelt refusing to shoot a cornered bear whilst on a hunt. A Russian immigrant named Morris Michtom was responsible for making a handmade 'Teddy Bear' and placing it in his shop window in New York. The response was amazing and the success of the idea is now history – the teddy bear was born! This company was licensed in 1953 to produce the 'Smokey Bear', a public awareness teddy bear for the US forestry commission. In 1962 Lionel A. Weintraub was appointed president, after twenty-one years with the company. By 1982 the company was sold to CBS Toys and by the mid 1980s, bears were no longer in production.

## Littlefolk

In 1976 in Devon, England, Graham McBride and Maggie Breedon started to produce soft toy animals in a 700-year-old mill. By 1980 they had produced their first teddy bear. These quality teddies were generally made from plush acrylic and were very popular. Mohair is still in demand today, particularly for the collectors' market. Sadly, Maggie Breedon died in 1991 and in the following year, Graham McBride formed a partnership with Possible Dreams Ltd in Massachusetts, USA.

## Merrythought

This company opened a spinning mill in Oakworth, Yorkshire, England in 1919 and in the 1920s it bought a mohair-weaving factory from Dyson Hall &

Co of Huddersfield. It registered the Merrythought trademark in 1930 and production of soft toys was soon in full swing – in fact, by the mid 1930s the company was said to be the largest producer of soft toys in all of Britain! During World War II, the factory was engaged in war work, making maps for the Admiralty. After this period the company, like many others in the post-war years, saw steady growth and recruited many well-known designers in the teddy bear world to join its ranks. The company's success has evolved into another well-known name in the teddy bear world, boosted by the increased interest in the adult collectors' bear market. Merrythought today boasts a healthy business, with a permanent shop and museum in its home town of Ironbridge, Telford in Shropshire, England.

## House of Nisbet

Peggy Nisbett started this company in 1955 in her home town of Weston-super-Mare in England. Her products at the time were dolls and it was not until the mid 1970s that teddy bears were produced in quantity. The famous 'Bully' bears of Peter Bull fame, along with his books, became a good trading foundation for House of Nisbet. In 1987 the company invented distressed mohair, in conjunction with Norton (Weaving) Ltd. This process was achieved by using an old velvet-crushing machine dating back to 1904! In 1989, Dakin Inc acquired the share capital.

## Peacock

This London company, founded in 1853, made wooden games and toys and it was not until the 1930s that teddy bears were in fairly large scale production. This was short-lived, however, as Peacock was purchased by Chad Valley in 1931. Chad Valley continued to market the Peacock teddy bear but by the end of that decade this practise ceased and the Peacock label was but a memory.

## Pedigree

Originally this company was founded around 1850 by two brothers George and Joseph Lines, making wooden toys and perambulators (baby carriages). The three sons of Joseph established Lines Bros Ltd in 1919 and after a move to a new factory in Merton, London they established a new trademark called Tri-Ang, a triangular symbol to represent the three brothers. They continued the manufacture of their toys, rocking horses and prams. Later, in 1931, these prams were to have their own trademark of 'Pedigree' – another well-known name today. In the mid to late 1930s, the Pedigree teddy bear started to evolve and this continued well into the 1950s when these bears were perhaps at their peak. However, this famous company suffered various set-backs and ceased trading in the late 1980s.

## Steiff

No teddy bear book has probably ever failed to mention Steiff, as this world-renowned German manufacturer is probably the most famous of all the manufacturers of teddy bears. Started by Margarete Steiff in 1877 in Giengen, Germany with a felt business it soon turned to making animals. Her nephew Richard joined the company as a designer in 1897 to expand the range of the soft toys, which were, at this time, still animals. Between 1902 and 1905 he experimented with a jointed bear design and the first registered design was Bar 35 Pab, which was registered on 12 February 1905. The success of the bear was absolutely phenomenal and the factory was expanded three times over a six-year period just to keep up! As with all manufacturing industries, growth halted during World War II and Steiff were diverted to making munitions. By the 1950s however, things were taking off again and in 1953 the company celebrated the 50th anniversary of the teddy bear. In 1980 it produced the first replica bear for the new collectors' market and from there on the floodgates opened. Today this company continues to flourish to become possibly the biggest teddy bear manufacturer of all time.

# Suppliers

### Bridon Bears & Friends

Brian & Donna Gibbs
'Bears Cottage',
42 St Michael's Lane,
Bridport, Dorset, DT6 3RD, UK
Tel/Fax: 01308 420796
www.bridonbears.force9.co.uk
www.bbears.fsnet.co.uk

As well as being authors of this book,
Brian and Donna design and produce
an extensive range of teddy bear kits
and patterns and also offer general bear
making supplies world-wide (all major
credit cards accepted). Full details on
website

### Admiral Bear Supplies

37 Warren Drive, Ruislip,
Middlesex, HA4 9RD, UK
Tel/Fax: 020 8868 9598
www.admiral-bears.com

### Fred Aldous Ltd

PO Box 135,
37 Lever Street,
Manchester, M60 1UX, UK
Tel: 0161 236 2477
Fax: 0161 236 6075
www.fredaldous.co.uk

### Barenstubchen Blummel

PO Box 610139 D-68231
Mannheim, Germany
Tel: 621-4838812
Fax: 621-4838820
www.baerenstuebchen.de

### Edinburgh Imports Ltd

PO Box 722
Woodland Hills,
California 91365-0722, USA
www.edinburgh.com

### The Glass Eye Co

School Bank Road,
Llanrwst, Gwynedd,
LL26 0HU, UK
Tel: 01492 642220
Fax: 01492 641643
www.glasseyes.com

### A Helmbold GmbH

Pluschweberei und Farberei,
D-98634 Oberweid,
Haupstrasse 44, Germany
Tel: 036946-22009
Fax: 036946-22020

# Acknowledgments

The authors, Brian and Donna, would like to give grateful thanks to the following: Jenny Nelson of Admiral Bear Supplies for supplying various fabrics, components and accessories used throughout this book.Fred Aldous Ltd for supplying all of the joints and polyester fillings used throughout.All of the staff at David & Charles who put up with us so courageously! Dave Wilkinson for his loyal support and finally to Dave Borley of Computer Solutions, 44 St Michael's Lane, Bridport, Dorset DT6 3RD, for sorting out our far-too-frequent computer problems!

# Further Reading

## Books

***The Big Bear Book*** Hockenberry (Schiffer, 1996)
Over 400 bears and their makers. Steiff-Chad Valley etc. US price guide.

***Enchanting Friends*** Hockenberry (Schiffer, 1995)
Collectible Poohs, Raggedies, Golliwogs and Roosevelt Bears. Major work on the history of these characters. US price guide too. 625 colour photos.

***More Enchanting Friends*** Hockenberry (Schiffer, 1998)
Superb sequel to *Enchanting Friends*. Lots more of everything and over fifty pages devoted to Golliwogs. Also includes Paddington.

***Restoring Teddy Bears and Stuffed Animals***
Pistorius (Portfolio Press, 2001)
From simple pad repairs to restoring a face and re-stuffing with excelsior. Full of colour and examples, plus material requirements (English).

***Steiff Bears & Other Playthings, Past & Present***
Hockenberry (Schiffer, 2000)
Massive work featuring many of the items made by Steiff. Includes identification and US price guide. Full colour.

***Teddy Bears and Friends Identification and Price Guide*** Mullins (Hobby House Press, 2000)
Current guide, also covers soft toys and animals from Europe, Japan, Australia and USA. Includes Chad Valley, Farnell, Merrythought & Steiff.

***Teddy Bears Past and Present*** Linda Mullins (Hobby House Press, 1989)

***Christie's Century of Teddy Bears*** Leyla Maniera (Pavilion Books, 2001)

***Miller's Teddy Bears – A Complete Collector's Guide*** Sue Pearson (Miller's Publications, 2001)

All of the titles opposite should be available direct and via mail order from:

**The Mulberry Bush**
9 George Street, Brighton,
East Sussex, BN2 1RH, UK
Tel: 01273 600471/493781
Fax: 01273 495138
Email: mulberry@mulberrybush.com
Website: www.mulberrybush.com

***Hugglets UK Teddy Bear Guide***
An annual publication that is an invaluable resource for bear makers everywhere. Filled with contact names and addresses for bear making supplies and stockists of manufacturers and artist bears. Mostly aimed at the UK but there is a small international section. Also published is a similar annual guide for the doll maker called *The UK Doll Directory*.
Hugglets
PO Box 290, Brighton, BN2 1DR, UK
Tel: 01273 697974
Fax: 01273 626255
Email: clarion@pavilion.co.uk

**Portfolio Press**
This American company has published several teddy bear related books, including:
*The World's Most Lovable Bears*, Stephen L. Cronk (a past editor of *Teddy Bear Review*), and
*A Celebration of Steiff: Timeless Toys for Today*, Krystyna Poray-Goddu (a past editorial director of *Teddy Bear Review*).
Portfolio Press is located at:
130 Wineow St, Cumberland, MD 21502, USA
Tel: (301) 724-2795
Fax: (301) 724-2796

# Magazines

### Teddy Bear Club International
Full colour monthly magazine with regular articles on teddy bear artists, old bears and patterns plus news pages for all that's new in the teddy bear world. Available world-wide and by subscription.
TBCI Magazine
Aceville Publications Ltd,
Castle House, 97 High Street, Colchester,
Essex, CO1 1TH, UK
Tel: 01206 505978
Website: www.planet-teddybear.com

### Teddy Bear Scene
A full colour, bi-monthly publication available on news-stands and through subscription world-wide. Exclusive features and editorial news, what's new, book and product reviews, museum reports, auction updates and old bear articles. (Also publishers of *Dolls House & Miniature Scene.*)
EMF Publishing
5–7 Elm Park, Ferring,
West Sussex BN12 5RN, UK
Tel: 01903 244900
Fax: 01903 506626
Email: dolltedemf@aol.com
Website: www.dolltedemf.com

### Teddy Bear Times
A monthly magazine in full colour containing regular articles, reviews, patterns and competitions. Available on news-stands and by subscription world-wide. Also publishers of *Doll Magazine*.
Ashdown Publishing
Avalon Court, Star Road, Partridge Green,
West Sussex, RH13 8RY, UK
Tel: 01403 711511
Fax: 01403 711521
Email: ashdown@ashdown.co.uk
Website: www.teddybeartimes.com

### Australian Folk Art Books
This magazine contains some of the many titles available including, *Australian Bear Creations* and *Dolls, Bears and Collectable's*, as well as occasional teddy bear special editions and books of bear patterns. Very informative with practical articles and editorial. Full colour throughout. Published by:
Express Lifestyle Publications
2 Stanley Street, Silverwater,
NSW 2128 Australia
Tel: (02) 9748 0599
Fax: (02) 9748 1956
Email: subs@expresspublications.com.au
Website: www.expresspublications.com.au

The UK Distibutors of Australian Folk Art Books can be found at:
4 The Long Yard, Wickfield,
Shefford Woodlands,
Berkshire RG17 7EH, UK
Tel: 01488 649955
Fax: 01488 649950
Email: heather@folkart.demon.co.uk

### Teddy Bear Review
1107 Broadway, Suite 1210 North,
New York, NY 10010
Tel (editorial offices): (212) 989-8700
Tel (subscription services): (614) 382-3322
Fax: (212) 645-8976
Email: rp@collector-online.com

# Museums

The following is a list of museums containing items of interest to the bear lover, including a shop in many cases. Whilst we appreciate that this listing is far from comprehensive, the museums mentioned are just a small representation of the widespread appeal of the teddy bear. Before visiting any museum it is wise to contact them first for opening times and so on.

## Europe

**Spielzeugmuseum**, Burgerspitalgasse 2, A-5020 Salzburg, Austria. Tel: 0043-662-84-75-60
**Musée du Jouet**, Rue de l'Association, 24 1000 Brussels, Belgium. Tel: 02-219-61-68
**St Goar am Rhein**, Deutchland Puppenmuseum. Sonnegasse 8, D-56329 St Goar, Germany. Tel: +49-6741-7270
**Puppenhausmuseum Basel**, Steinenvorstadt 1, CH-4051 Basel, Germany. Tel: +41 (0) 61 225 95 95
**Margarete Steiff Museum**, Alleenstrasse, Giengen, Germany. Tel: 07322-131-0

## United Kingdom/Ireland

**The Bear Museum**, 38 Dragon Street, Petersfield, Hampshire GU31 4JJ. Tel: 01730 265108
**Bethnal Green Museum of Childhood**, Cambridge Heath Road, London E2 9PA. Tel: 0208 983 5200
**The Bournemouth Bears**, Expocentre, Old Christchurch Lane, Bournemouth BH1 1NE. Tel: 01202 293544
**Broadway Bears Museum**, 76 High Street, Broadway, Worcs WR12 7AJ. Tel: 01386 858323
**Ironbridge Toy Museum**, Ironbridge, Shropshire TF8 7NJ. Tel: 01952 433029
**Hamilton Toy Collection**, 111 Main St, Callander, Perthshire FK17 8BQ. Tel: 018773 30004
**Museum of Childhood**, 42 High Street, Edinburgh EH1 1TG. Tel: 0131 5294142
**Museum of Childhood Memories**, 1 Castle Street, Beaumaris, Anglesey, Gwynedd LL58 8AP. Tel: 01248 712498
**The London Toy and Model Museum**, 21–23 Craven Hill, London W2 3EN. Tel: 020 7706 8000
**Park House**, Park St, Stow-on the-Wold, Gloucestershire GL54 1AQ. Tel: 01451 830159
**Pollock's Toy Museum**, 1 Scala Street, London W1P 1LT. Tel: 020 7636 3452
**The British Bear Collection**, Banwell Castle, Banwell, Somerset BS29 6NX. Tel: 01934 822263
**Teddy Bear House**, Antelope Walk, Dorchester, Dorset DT1 1BE. Tel: 01305 263200
**The Teddy Bear Museum**, 19 Greenhill Street, Stratford-upon-Avon, Warwickshire CV37 6LF. Tel: 01789 293160
**Toy and Teddy Bear Museum**, 373 Clifton Drive North, St Annes, Lancashire FY8 2PA. Tel: 01253 713705

## America

**Teddy Bear Castle Museum**, 203 South Pine, Nevada City, California 95959. Tel: 530-265-5804
**Teddy Bear Museum of Naples**, 2511 Pine Ridge Road, Naples, Florida 34109. Tel: 941-598-2711
**Children's Museum of Indianapolis**, 3000 N. Meridian Street, Indianapolis, Indiana, IN 46208-4716. Tel: 317-334-3322
**Aunt Len's Doll and Toy Museum**, 6 Hamilton Terrace, New York City, New York 10031. Tel: 212-281-4143
**Theodore Roosevelt Birthplace**, 28 East 20th Street, New York City, New York, 10003. Tel: 212-260-1616

# INDEX